Problem Drinking
Experiments in Detoxification

Report of the Detoxification
Evaluation Project

Bedford Square Press | NCVO

Published by
BEDFORD SQUARE PRESS of the
National Council for Voluntary Organisations
26 Bedford Square, London WC1B 3HU

ISBN 0 7199 1115 X

First published 1985

Typeset by
Acorn Bookwork, Salisbury, Wiltshire
Printed and bound in England by
Henry Ling Ltd
at the Dorset Press,
Dorchester, Dorset

Contents

Acknowledgements

The Detoxification Evaluation Project research team would like to thank the following people for their support and assistance: Sir Desmond Pond, MD, FRCP, PRCP, project supervisor while Professor of Psychiatry, the London Hospital; the DHSS Homelessness and Addictions Research Liaison Group; Phoebe Hall and Vince Keddie, DHSS research liaison officers; DEP research assistants Stephen Farnfield, Janet Leadbitter, Barbara Lopko, Angela Sparrowhawk and Philippa Webster; consultants Dr Alan Cartwright and Dr Alan Smith; DEP office staff, in particular, Diane Harding and Jane Cookman; Dr Jim Orford, Nina Little and Ken Edwards.

We are particularly grateful for the help and co-operation given to us by the staff and clients of the detoxification centres.

This research was funded by the Department of Health and Social Services. However, the views expressed are those of the research team and are not necessarily those of the DHSS.

Members of the Research Team

Landy Hashimi
Shirley Otto
Stan Shaw

1
Introduction

This book is based on research which the authors were commissioned to undertake on five examples of detoxification services: in Leeds, Manchester, Oxford, Tower Hamlets in the East End of London, and Portsmouth. The first two, Leeds and Manchester, were originally intended to deal exclusively with persons arrested for public drunkenness and brought to the centre by the police. The next two, Oxford and Tower Hamlets, dealt with persons referred by themselves or community agents other than the police. In Portsmouth, persons were dealt with in the general admission wards of a psychiatric hospital which had no special setting for detoxification per se.

The original aim was to evaluate these centres, working on the assumption that they would be relatively similar and have definable and comparable goals. Early visits to the different detoxification centres soon revealed that this was far from the case. The five different institutions which all called themselves 'detoxification centres' varied immensely in their methods, staffing, facilities, goals and clientele.

For example, one was a purpose-built unit in a psychiatric hospital staffed by a consultant psychiatrist, psychologist, three registrars, nursing officer, seven other nurses and six nursing assistants; another centre comprised some converted rooms behind a Salvation Army lodging-house supervised by a nurse, who was the solitary full-time member of staff. One centre prescribed the tranquiliser Heminevrin as a matter of course; another centre had a policy of *never* prescribing any drugs if at all possible. One centre's policy was to accept only referrals of drunken persons brought by the police; another centre would usually refuse to admit anyone brought drunk!

Of course, any socio-medical problem could be approached in different ways. But it soon became apparent that these places were not even dealing with the same sorts of client, or attempting to achieve the same things. Since the research aim was to compare these places, it became pressing to try and establish some core goals, some common ground which was unquestionably the business of detoxification. Initial thinking was to centre the concept of detoxification around a core clinical state. If detoxification centres were any-

1

thing, surely they would be places attempting to deal with the effects
of withdrawal from alcohol. Yet even this seemed inappropriate
once data on the first centre were collected. This centre was designed
for homeless habitual drunkenness offenders, but staff during
piloting reported that during their stay in the centre, virtually none of
the clients displayed any withdrawal symptoms, even though very
few were prescribed any drugs. Did this mean that this institution
was not a detoxification centre at all? The staff there would have
claimed that the more important goals of detoxification centres lay in
the wider questions of diverting their clients from the penal system,
and eventually extracting them from their rootless, drink-centred
life-style. From this one might suspect that different uses of the term
'detoxification' merely reflected biases between different professional groups. This would probably be partly true, but would not by
itself account for the inconsistency in the use of this term. In discussing the subject with staff in hospital settings, great differences were
found just amongst doctors as to what they took detoxification to
mean. To some, it was solely the effects of acute withdrawal from
alcohol, whilst to others it was much more concerned with the
question of helping problem drinkers to refrain from abusing alcohol
in the long term. Doctors who did not specialise in drink problems
did not use the word 'detoxification' in either of these senses. To
them, *de-toxifying* was primarily treating the intake or overdose of a
toxic substance (rather than an addictive substance), and they usually related the term to drugs, chemicals or poisons rather than to
alcohol.

   In discussing the possible opening of future detoxification centres
in other areas the authors found planners from all professional
groups to have little clear idea of exactly what they wanted a
detoxification centre to do, for whom, or why. The notion of opening a detoxification centre seemed often to be an idealised goal which
it was assumed would magically fill all existing gaps in the local
pattern of services. Without wishing to douse enthusiasm, it seemed
high time that a critical look was taken at the idea of detoxification
and detoxification centres to see how these terms acquired their
current chameleon-like manifestations, to disentangle them into
more workable ideas which might lead to clearer planning of treatment and services.

What is detoxification?

There was even confusion about the very word 'detoxification'.
Firstly, some people in the field would claim that it is more proper
and correct to spell the word 'detoxication'. It might mean the state
a person is in as alcohol leaves the body, or it might mean some-

thing that is done to them or for them in this state. Throughout this report we have used 'detoxication' to mean the condition and 'detoxification' to mean the treatment.

Not surprisingly, then, definitions of detoxification usually impart vague notions of both meanings. For example, the report of the working party on habitual drunkenness offenders (Weiler, 1971) 'defines' detoxification thus:

> Detoxification involves in the first instance the simple process of sobering up. In those subjects who are physiologically dependent on alcohol, withdrawal symptoms must then also be treated.

This 'definition' is typical in that it creates as many problems as it solves. It leaves one to wonder in what way is detoxification actually different from sobering up? Do people who are not dependent have no withdrawal symptoms? Do withdrawal symptoms always require 'treatment'?

The definition begs these questions because 'detoxification' is being defined in terms of various constituent elements which are not themselves specified. To clarify matters, each of these constituent elements must be considered in turn. In the first place, detoxification, in the sense of an acute state, must be a state of 'reaction' to a previous condition of intoxification. Indeed, some detoxification centres, particularly those dealing with persons arrested for drunkenness, were found to spend a large part of their time managing persons in a state of intoxication rather than detoxification. But although concepts about detoxification are usually ideas about the after-effects of intoxification, this essential proceeding stage is not usually considered.

What is intoxication?

When alcohol is consumed, it is absorbed into the stomach and intestine and then into the blood stream, via which it is distributed throughout the body. As alcohol in the blood stream flows into the brain, it affects the central nervous system, vision, co-ordination and muscular activities. At low blood alcohol concentrations, it acts as a central nervous system stimulant, but as a depressant at higher concentrations. However, even concentrations as low as below 50 mg/100 ml may alter mood (Gross, M. M., 1977). The peak of intoxication is the point at which the concentration of alcohol in the blood is at its highest. This does not happen immediately after alcohol intake. For example, after a single drink the concentration of alcohol in the blood will rise to a peak between thirty minutes and an hour after the drink was consumed. However, any intake of alcohol, however small, has some degree of pharmacological effect, and so technically speaking, any intake of alcohol can be said to produce a degree of intoxication. It is therefore necessary to distinguish this term, 'intoxication' from 'drunkenness'.

Drunkenness

Drunkenness is the common term usually applied to a state of relatively pronounced intoxication. The term 'drunk' is usually applied to a person whose intoxication has reached a level sufficient to produce observable alterations in mood and behaviour. Drunkenness is typically caused by a larger or quicker alcohol intake than is usual for the drinker. The degree of drunkenness depends not only on the amount of alcohol ingested, and the length of time over which it was consumed, but also on other factors such as whether the person had eaten beforehand.

Intoxication is sometimes taken to mean drunkenness, but technically, intoxication could be said to begin as soon as consumed alcohol enters the blood stream, and not to conclude until this alcohol leaves the blood stream. Thus, a period of intoxication can last longer than a period of obvious drunkenness. For example, a person weighing 8 to 10 stone, who drank eight pints of bitter during the evening might not appear drunk the following morning but would still very likely fail the police breath test. In this sense, it is reasonable to consider that a person can be intoxicated without being drunk.

The process of *intoxication* should be distinguished from the process of *metabolism* of alcohol. Metabolism of alcohol means the body breaking down and getting rid of the alcohol taken in. This process begins immediately alcohol is ingested and continues until all consumed alcohol has left the body. Whatever the amount consumed, the body metabolises alcohol at a fairly steady rate of about 50 mg/100 ml per hour. Alcohol is eliminated mostly by oxidation, but also via the breath and urine. The process of *metabolism*, by which the body *gets rid of the alcohol intake*, must be distinguished from the ways in which the body *reacts to having been intoxicated*. These after-effects might be the reaction to one relatively short episode of intoxication, or the reaction to numerous episodes of intoxication which may have had cumulative effects.

Broadly speaking, there are two areas of psycho-biological after-effect. These are:

Withdrawal symptoms — the psychological and physical reactions to the effect of alcohol as a tranquiliser

These begin to occur as blood alcohol concentration starts to drop. They can be relatively mild, such as slight mood disturbance and disturbed sleep, or be relatively severe, such as bodily shakes and hallucinations. Withdrawal symptoms can be conceptualised in the following way: alcohol has a sedative effect upon the central nervous system, i.e. it depresses and slows it down. Thus, when blood alcohol concentration starts to drop, the system slightly over-reacts and becomes more agitated and active than usual. It can be thought of as a defensive response by the central nervous system called into place to counteract the ability of alcohol to depress brain activity. To quote the Royal College of Psychiatrists' report, *Alcohol and Alcoholism* (1979, p. 47):

> The processes that have countered depression of brain activity in the presence of alcohol cause a surge of excitation when alcohol is removed. The analogy might be with the door that has a person on one side pushing it, and on the other side someone holding it shut . . . suddenly stop holding it shut, and the pushing of the other person now sends the door flying open with great energy.

Since any alcohol intake leading to a blood concentration of 50 mg/100 ml and above causes some degree of depression of the brain's activity, there might always be some degree of central nervous system excitation as blood alcohol levels fall. So just as any intake of alcohol produces a degree of intoxication, this will, in turn, always be followed by some degree of withdrawal. Of course, mild symptoms, although sometimes uncomfortable, are not dangerous, and only more severe withdrawals require a specific medical response. These are conceptually, though not always practically, distinguishable from:

The physical reactions to the toxic effect of alcohol as a poison

Alcoholic drinks contain ethyl alcohol, which is toxic. It can cause physical upset to various parts of the body. The reaction to having ingested a toxic substance can occur after a single episode of intoxication, such as nausea and vomiting, or might follow numerous episodes of intoxication which have had cumulative effects, such as chronic liver damage, alcoholic hepatitis, peripheral neuritis, and acute inflammation of the brain and dementia. Some reactions to high intoxication, such as acute gastric erosion or acute pancreatitis, can be life-threatening. All these require specific medical responses, but treatment cannot repair damage in all cases.

In such chronic cases, a person's condition might also be due to problems which are not directly effects of alcohol per se. For example, vitamin deficiency is typical of hospitalised alcoholics, but besides the direct effect of alcohol per se, this has usually been compounded by the disorganised life-style of problem drinkers.

Moreover, some research suggests that sustained high concentrations of alcohol also increase the levels of other poisonous substances (Gross, 1977).

Hangover

There are various other terms sometimes used to refer to the effects of intoxication. Like drunkenness, 'hangover' is a commonly used term which has no specific technical meaning. A hangover is a combination of (usually mild) withdrawal symptoms, in combination with reaction to the physical effects of alcohol as a poison. Thus, in a typical hangover, sleep disturbance or slight anxiety may be the withdrawal symptoms, and nausea and vomiting might be the physical reaction. Hangovers can occur before the end of the processes of metabolism and intoxication, i.e. hangovers can begin while there is still alcohol in the blood stream.

A hangover is also caused by other factors apart from alcohol ingestion. For example, headaches are often thought to be created as much by the congeners, i.e. addition substances in alcoholic drinks which give colour and taste, as by the alcohol itself. Hangovers can be aggravated by having had little sleep, and by guilt and remorse for the previous night's behaviour.

Sobering up and drying out

These two terms cannot be precisely distinguished from each other. Sobering up usually means the process of reaction to one relatively short episode of intoxication and usually occurs during the same stage as a hangover. It typically comprises overcoming relatively mild withdrawal symptoms such as disturbed sleep and anxiety, and physical reaction to alcohol intake such as thirst and nausea.

Drying out usually means the process of reaction to cumulative or lengthy episodes of intoxication. There may be physical upsets which last for some while, such as gastritis. There may be more chronic damage such as liver damage and ulceration. There are likely to be more significant withdrawal symptoms.

Although no precise distinction can be made between sobering up and drying out, the term 'drying out' usually refers to a more extreme and complex case than 'sobering up'. In every-day parlance, people might refer to anyone who has been drunk as sobering up, but would be unlikely to apply the term 'drying out' to everyone. Drying out usually means a person recovering from either a particularly extreme episode of intoxication, or a period of chronic or recurrent intoxication.

What is detoxification?

Where does the term 'detoxification' fit into all this? The answer is, virtually anywhere and everywhere.

By detoxification, some doctors mean only the effects of alcohol or other drugs as toxic substances. Others apply the term only to cases of severe withdrawal. Some place the major emphasis of detoxification treatment on the patient's general physical condition. Detoxification sometimes refers in a passive sense to a person's condition, sometimes in an active sense to the response to such a person. So who is to say which particular medical definition of detoxification would be most appropriate?

Doubtless any doctor reading this report might well think he or she could provide a working definition of detoxification, but the authors guarantee that an equally qualified doctor could be found who would disagree with the definition and in some cases, the discrepancies would be extreme. Moreover, many people working in the detoxification services do not define detoxification and detoxification services in terms of medical criteria at all. Some believe that the medical effects of alcohol per se are easily managed side issues, and the real aims of detoxification are to persuade people with drinking problems to give up their habits, to become rehabilitated into more settled life-styles or to break their pattern of drunkenness offences.

Indeed, one could go on pointing out many different activities carried out in the name of 'detoxification', which will be described in the main body of the book. For the present, it can only be said that the term 'detoxification' actually has no precise clinical meaning: it is an ambiguous umbrella term which may or may not be taken to include a variety of constituent processes. It may or may not also include non-medical concepts.

It may seem ironic that at the beginning of a book on detoxification the first suggestion should be that the term 'detoxification' does not have a precise meaning. However, this is meant in all seriousness and is not proposed merely to be controversial. Indeed it seems to the authors that much of the controversy over detoxification, the extreme positions sometimes taken and the lack of a consistent plan for services for either drunkenness offenders and/or people suffering withdrawal symptoms, have arisen precisely because of the very considerable misunderstandings over terminology, and the difficulties over planning a response when it seems that everyone is talking at cross purposes about quite different things.

The situation is in fact very much like that regarding the term 'alcoholism', which became a term involving so many different concepts, that it gradually came to have no precise meaning at all. It created difficulties in organising a response to what was actually a range of varied problems. Accordingly, the term fell into disfavour. Various attempts were made to distinguish instead the constituent elements such as degrees of dependence, and alcohol-related problems. Probably the term 'detoxification' has arrived at the same stage of confusion, and attempts are beginning to be made to talk instead about particular elements within it. For example, Scottish documents no longer refer to 'detoxification centres' but simply to 'designated places', thus clearly defining the agencies in terms of their working system as places designated by the Secretary of State as somewhere the police can take drunkenness offenders, and avoiding all the connotations of detoxification. Clearly this begs the following question:

What is a detoxification centre?

Since the agencies in Leeds, Manchester, Tower Hamlets and Oxford all called themselves detoxification centres, it is simplest for this book to comply. However, their clientele, staffing and modes of operation were all radically different. There were two major distinguishing characteristics. Firstly, some detoxification centres were based in a hospital setting and others were not. Secondly, some were 'designated' as centres to which the police could take persons arrested for drunkenness offences, whilst others were not. These two distinctions effectively made the four specialist services to be considered all unique since:
• Leeds was a designated non-hospital detoxification centre
• Manchester was a designated hospital detoxification centre
• Oxford was a non-designated hospital detoxification centre
• Tower Hamlets was a non-designated non-hospital detoxification centre.

BACKGROUND TO THE PROJECT

Drunkenness and the law

Drunkenness is a relatively common phenomenon. In a 1974 general population survey (Cartwright, 1975), 27 per cent of adults reported having been drunk at some point in the previous 12 months. Most instances of drunkenness do not present any significant social or physical problems, although of course it can lead to accidents, petty crime and so forth. Sometimes, then, drunkenness can lead a drunken person to become a danger to himself/herself and an embarrassment or danger to others. So in English law, whilst drunkenness itself is not a legal offence, it becomes so when it is exhibited in 'a highway or other public place whether a building or not, or on any licensed premises' (s. 12 of the Licensing Act 1872). Moreover, the drunken person can only be arrested if he is considered incapable of taking care of himself, and virtually all proceedings for 'simple drunkenness', usually referred to as 'drunk and incapable', follow this particular charge. Besides simple drunkenness, there are various offences in English law in which drunkenness in public occurs with other forms of anti-social behaviour. This series of laws is usually referred to collectively as 'aggravated drunkenness'. The most common of these is the charge of being guilty, while drunk, of riotous or disorderly behaviour, and this is usually referred to as 'drunk and disorderly'. Of the other aggravated offences, the most familiar is being 'drunk and indecent', which actually refers to various slightly differing nineteenth-century statutes.

Although the law relating to drunkenness in this form dates back to s. 12 of the Licensing Act of 1872, virtually as soon as these laws were passed, there arose a feeling that perhaps punishment was not the most appropriate response for all persons who committed these offences, particularly those who habitually committed such offences. Such offenders were the subject of a government inquiry in 1879, which put forward the idea of special treatment centres for habitual public drunks, as an alternative to the usual fines and/or imprisonment. Indeed, following the Inquiry's recommendations, the 1879 Habitual Drunkenness Act and the 1898 Inebriate Act provided for compulsory committal of habitual drunkards to special homes. However, these Acts were never of much effect, partly due to a lack of belief in compulsion, but more importantly due to those two persistent reasons, a shortage of funds, and a division of responsibility between local and central government.

Furthermore, this strict application of reduced hours of opening for licensed premises during the First World War meant that by the end of the war, the number of drunkenness offences was only one-sixth the level it had been four years previously. The problem of public drunkenness was temporarily shelved.

It re-emerged with some consequence in the 1960s, as the economic and legal situation changed drastically. The 1961 Licensing Act, the abolition of resale price maintenance in 1967, and a host of other compounding social and economic circumstances meant that the real price of alcohol fell drastically during a period when alcohol became increasingly more available through wider distribution outlets. The result was a considerable rise in the consumption of alcohol throughout the population, creating accompanying rises in the prevalence of alcohol-related problems (Shaw, 1980). Conspicuous amongst these problems was a rising rate of public drunkenness. By the mid 1960s there were over 80,000 drunkenness convictions annually from which approximately 3,000 imprisonments a year resulted. Since crime in general was rising and many more persons were being sent to over-crowded prisons, the question rose again as to whether drunkenness offenders should be processed through the courts and prisons.

However, this question was discussed not in terms of the economic and legal circumstances which had created this situation, but rather in terms of the behaviour of drunkenness offenders. In particular, this reflected the prevailing conceptualisation of drinking problems at that time, a conceptualisation which had not arisen because of experiences in Britain, but from experiences in America.

In Britain, widespread public drunkenness was suddenly curtailed by the introduction of licensing laws during the First World War. In America, this had not happened and the situation had become increasingly worse. Eventually, the pressure of the Temperance Movements became so great that total prohibition of alcohol was instituted. Although many alcohol-related problems naturally declined during Prohibition, including public drunkenness, Prohibition proved highly unpopular, and became associated with organised violent crime. Thus a new response to alcohol problems had to be found which appeared in the public mind as having nothing to do with large-scale legal restriction or the drinking habits of the majority. At the end of the prohibition era, the emergence of Alcoholics Anonymous fitted this bill exactly. AA claimed that alcohol itself was not the problem and that most drinkers were not susceptible to drinking problems. The only problem lay in a particular group of drinkers who were physically and psychologically allergic to alcohol. Although there was no firm scientific evidence for this concept, the notion that all alcohol problems could be attributed to a minority of people with an illness was very attractive to Americans just after Prohibition. AA grew greatly in size, and its view of alcohol problems was accepted on a widespread scale, spreading to Europe just after the Second World War. Indeed, during this period, the notion that a minority of people had a disease called alcoholism completely dominated thinking about alcohol problems (Shaw, 1982).

Thus it was that in Britain in the 1960s, planners and providers of services did not see themselves as responding to alcohol problems in general, but only saw themselves responding in a narrow way to the very evident problems of a core group of 'alcoholics'. The question of public drunkenness was no exception. The reaction to the rises in public drunkenness did not consider the economic distribution of alcohol, changes in social behaviour generally, or even the behaviour of all drunkenness offenders as a group. Rather 'treating the habitual drunken offender in effect means treating the disease of alcoholism' (Weiler Report, p. 183).

This is at the source of the ambiguity and confusion about

detoxification and detoxification centres, and the continual shifting of responses to public drunkenness without an analysis of the causal factors involved or assessment of the expected efficiency of various potential responses.

The most recent of these attempted responses can be traced back to the crucial watershed year of 1967. In that year, s. 91 (1) of the Criminal Justice Act provided for the abolition of imprisonment as a penalty for the offence of being drunk and disorderly, but stated that this change would not be implemented 'unless the Secretary of State of the day is satisfied that sufficient suitable accommodation is available for the care and treatment of persons convicted of being drunk and disorderly' (s. 91 (5)). Thus no distinction was made between 'drunk and disorderly' offenders who would need treatment and those who would not. The response to all offenders had become mixed up with the idea of responding to some offenders who were presumed sick. Thus, introducing the second reading in the House of Lords of the Criminal Justice Act 1967, Lord Stonham stated that

> the work of drying out and cleaning up these men, well knowing that they will soon be back in prison, is a stupid waste of our badly strained prison resources, particularly at prisons like Pentonville, where drunks account for one in six of all admissions. Neither the excellent clinic there nor the fresh air we provide at Springhill open prison is a substitute for the continuous support these sick people need if they are to be, at least partially, restored to useful citizenship. Prison is not the place.

This quote points to three major aims which were presumed necessary in improving the response to public drunkenness. These were:

1 Habitual drunkenness offenders should be diverted from courts and prisons and instead sent into some sort of treatment system, as 'prison is not the place'. This philosophy is sometimes referred to as 'decriminalisation' or 'diversion'.
2 Habitual drunkenness offenders needed attention being paid to their immediate physical and psychological state— 'the work of drying out and cleaning up these men'.
3 There should be an attempt to encourage and support them to give up their existing life-style and habit of drunkenness and attempt to rehabilitate them to a more conventional life-style— 'the continuous support these sick people need if they are to be, at least partially, restored to useful citizenship'.

Thus, the 'suitable accommodation within the community for the care and treatment of persons convicted of drunkenness offences' required by the Home Secretary in order to implement s. 91 of the Criminal Justice Act 1967, became conceptualised as places which would attempt to fulfil these three major aims.

The consideration of the range of treatment facilities available for this group of offenders, and the range of alternatives that might be created, become pressing.

Report of the working party on habitual drunken offenders (Weiler Report)

So 1967 also saw the appointment of a working party, under the chairmanship of Mr T. G. Weiler,

> to consider the treatment, within the penal system, of offenders who were habitually committing offences involving drunkenness, to assess the extent and nature of the need for such treatment, including the use and provision of hostels, and to make recommendations.

Their report was published four years later. Although the major bulk of their work was concerned with assessing existing treatment arrangements, and a range of facilities, with particular attention to hostels, the committee also paid attention to the idea of detoxification centres. Since these are the subject of this book, considerable attention must be paid at this point to the report's views which were instrumental in the establishment of two of the detoxification centres considered herein. The Weiler Report envisaged that the treatment facilities acting as an alternative to the processing of habitual drunks through the penal system would be detoxification centres along the lines of previous experiments in Czechoslovakia, Sweden and North America, such that

> persons who under present arrangements would be arrested for being drunk in public should be taken by the police to a detoxification centre and there detained while they are dried out, and any necessary medical and social investigations carried out.

The working party's view was that the existing system of processing through the courts and prisons was nothing but token disapproval of public drunkenness, and that in the case of habitual offenders, imprisonment was an inefficient, inappropriate and impractical waste of prison resources. Attention was paid, as explained in the report's name, to *habitual* offenders, who were defined as those who committed three or more drunkenness offences within a 12-month period:

> We should note that neither our terms of reference nor the provisions embodied in section 91 of the Criminal Justice Act 1967 contemplate that drunkenness in public should cease to be an offence under English criminal law. None of our witnesses suggested such a change and we have not been aware of any body of opinion which would favour it. (*Weiler Report, 1971, 3.14*).

Since fines were mostly paid by non-habitual offenders, it was considered they should be kept. The core of the problem, it seemed to the working party, was the habitual drunkenness offender who invariably could not pay his or her fine. It was therefore concluded that some sort of special arrangement must be made for them. Given the strength of the disease concept of alcoholism at the time, it was presumed that they were habitual offenders because they were suffering from alcoholism. The Weiler Report stresses '*the fact* that repeated arrests for public drunkenness is often a symptom of the disease of alcoholism [our italic]' (1.3) and '*the fact* that alcoholism is widely accepted as a disease [our italic]' (2.20). It refers to increasing recognition that 'drunks who are continually passing through police stations, courts and prisons in many of the major cities of the world are "sick" rather than "bad"' (1.3). Therefore, the special arrangements considered for these offenders were basically methods of care and treatment then considered appropriate responses to the disease of alcoholism. It was presumed that amongst this group, the after-effects of drunkenness would be much more serious, and might involve severe withdrawal symptoms, and even possibly delirium tremens and convulsions. Indeed, it was stated that amongst habitual offenders 'Epileptiform convulsions and delirium tremens are complications of withdrawal which *not infrequently* arise [our italic]' (7.13).

It was further assumed that habitual drunkenness offenders invariably would be men of no fixed abode, and therefore treatment arrangements would be concerned with 'rehabilitation' in the widest sense.

Since the Weiler Report's recommendations on detoxification were important in shaping two of the detoxification centres described later, and since these descriptions contrast how detoxification centres actually operated compared to the prescriptions and suggestions put forward in the Weiler Report, its recommendations on detoxification as abbreviated in its summary of conclusions and recommendations are provided in appendix 4.

Experimental detoxification centres

In response to the Weiler Report's recommendations, s. 34 of the Criminal Justice Act 1972 empowered the police to take persons who were drunk and incapable or drunk and disorderly to a place approved by the Secretary of State as a 'medical treatment centre for alcoholics'. The next year, again following other recommendations in the Weiler Report and after consultation between the Home Office and the DHSS, the Home Secretary announced that departmental responsibility for the provision of facilities for habitual drunkenness offenders should pass to the DHSS. This brought official recognition that habitual drunkenness offenders should be taken out of the penal system and treated instead by health and social services (DHSS Circular 21/73, para 3).

Although the Weiler Report described a possible detoxification programme in some detail, it did not recommend what form the suggested pilot schemes should take. The working party admitted 'we have not ourselves been able to suggest a basis on which a pilot scheme could be carried out in advance of legislation' (15.51), mainly because their terms of reference were clearly to consider services provided 'within the penal system'. Whilst the Working Party mentioned the possibility of detoxification centres being financed by the Home Office, they felt this might create certain practical and administrative difficulties and they did not feel able to consider what alternative sources of funding there might be since 'we should have been going outside our terms of reference and involving ourselves in questions of priorities which . . . we do not regard ourselves as competent to assess (15.52).

The scene was thus set for a pilot detoxification experiment in either London or a provincial city; but the way they would be financed, managed and organised were open questions. Further-more, London, Birmingham, Nottingham and Liverpool had all been cited in the Weiler Report as possible locales for the pilot schemes, but the two experimental centres which eventually opened were in Leeds and Manchester. In some ways, these two cities fitted the requirements of the Weiler Report's expectations; in some ways they did not. They were both suitable places in terms of their rates of drunkenness arrests. The Greater Manchester and West Yorkshire police districts had always figured relatively highly in the annual lists of drunkenness offences, and both places were also known to have largish populations of men of no fixed abode. Both cities figured prominently in the migratory patterns of such men, being stopping-off points en route between London and Scotland. Indeed, the Weiler Report noted (8.31) that in 1970, St Georges Crypt – a night shelter in Leeds – had dealt with 100 to 180 men per night and 3,000 different men over the course of a year. Both cities fitted the Weiler Report's hopes that detoxification centres should be created where they could form part of an overall pattern of services. The initiative for establishing a detoxification centre in Leeds came from the St Anne's Shelter and Housing Action, a non-statutory project working with homeless men in Leeds which was already managing hostels and a day shelter. The initiative for a detoxification centre in Man-chester came from the Department of Psychiatry at Withington Hospital, which was already operating an Alcohol Treatment Unit, and whose staff were actively involved in the operation of various services for problem drinkers in Greater Manchester. Both projects managed to obtain the co-operation and support of the local police, which was also seen by the Weiler Report as essential to the opera-tion of such experiments.

Nevertheless there was some difference between their scale of operation and that envisaged in the Weiler Report. In an appendix to the Weiler Report, the police in the two cities gave evidence that they did not consider there were too many habitual drunkenness offenders in their district (see table 1.1).

Moreover the scale of the experiments envisaged by the Weiler Report was relatively unambitious. Members of the Working Party discussed with police chiefs ideas of limited experiments in which only drunk and incapable offenders would be involved and possibly charged in the normal way after drying out (15.49 and 15.50). They speculated that 'the provision necessary for this purpose alone (i.e. a detoxification service by itself) could be very modest' (15.53).

The scope of both experimental centres was wider than this. However, both centres were only opened after months of discussion over their funding and operation. Neither centre was opened until operational policies had been drawn out in considerable detail and accepted by the DHSS, local statutory authorities, local voluntary agencies, and the local police and probation services. Both operational policy documents follow relatively closely the Weiler Report recommendations, for full-scale detoxification programmes contained in the main body of the report (15.32–15.42). Both considered the services to be part of a range of treatment and rehabilitation services; both had relatively high inputs of well-qualified staff, which had been stressed within the Weiler Report's discussion (15.34–15.40).

The setting up of the Detoxification Evaluation Project (DEP)

As noted in recommendation 98 of the Weiler Report, the twin purposes of a pilot detoxification scheme would be to provide a basis for experimentation and research. The report noted that 'research must therefore be built into all new therapeutic endeavours so that their efficacy can be properly assessed' (9.13). The DHSS invited the

Table 1.1   Police evidence

	Approx. no. of HDOs* (3 + yr)			Approx. no. in each age group			% of those living rough
	M	F	Total	30	30–50	50+	
Leeds	15	7	22	2	16	4	70%
Manchester	66	1	67	8	44	15	90%

Source: Weiler Report, *Habitual Drunken Offenders: Report of the Working Party*, HMSO, 1971, appendix G
*HDO means habitual drunkenness offender

authors of this book to submit 'A Research Proposal for the Evaluation of Detoxification Services'. Following the acceptance of this
proposal, the Detoxification Evaluation Project (DEP) was funded
from July 1977. The project was based at the Maudsley Hospital,
and was supervised by Sir Desmond Pond, Professor of Psychiatry at
the London Hospital.

The initial terms of reference for the project were to study the two
experimental detoxification centres set up in response to the recommendations of the Weiler Report, with the presumption that a third
such centre eventually would be opened in London and added to the
project's focus of study. When DEP commenced, the Leeds
detoxification centre had actually been in operation for some 14
months, so initial piloting and research naturally concentrated on
this centre.

The changing of DEP's terms of reference

After a first interim report, it was felt that the remit of the research
should be reviewed for the following reasons:
1   The London-based experimental detoxification centre which
would have accepted police referrals of habitual drunkenness
offenders was unable to go ahead as planned.
2   By that time, the Leeds detoxification centre was actually nearing
the end of its experimental period of three years which the DHSS had
agreed to fund, and some preliminary conclusions were already
being drawn about which that centre had been designed to test.
3   On the other hand, the difference between the scale of operation
of the pilot detoxification experiments envisaged by the Weiler
Report and the more comprehensive detoxification centres which
had developed in practice had created a concern to explore the
possibly more common situations where less resources were available for detoxification. As the Weiler Report had noted in recommendation 96, 'the establishment of fully operational detoxification
centres will be possible only in a few cities where the extent and
pattern of drunkenness offences warrant it. Elsewhere the service
will have to be provided in other less specialised ways'.
4   The debate about the nature of drinking problems and how they
should be treated, discussed in the introduction, had continued in
flux since the publication of the Weiler Report, and indeed since the
opening of the Leeds detoxification centre. By the end of the 1970s,
informed opinion in the field of alcohol problems had reached a
consensus that plans should be disgarded which presumed the
required response was specialist services for a minority group of
heavily damaged drinkers who suffered the disease of alcoholism. In
1978, the publication of *The Pattern and Range of Services for
Problem Drinkers* by the Government's Advisory Committee on

Alcoholism emphatically endorsed the idea that the target population was no longer just 'alcoholics' but anyone whose drinking was causing them any sort of problem, and that the required response should not be based on specialist services but upon improved response across the board from a range of largely non-specialist services.

5   Since the publication of the Weiler Report and the Criminal Justice Act 1972, there also had been various adjustments to the law regarding drunkenness, particularly in 1977 and 1978, which had effectively increased fines but reduced the length of sentences for non-payment. These changes are presented in more detail in appendix 1.

Moreover, in keeping with the shift in conceptualisation, the Criminal Law Act 1977, schedule 12, referred back to s. 34 (1) of the 1972 Criminal Justice Act which had allowed the police to take drunkenness offenders to 'medical treatment centres'. The 1977 Act removed the word 'medical' from this sentence.

All these changing factors created a growing concern to consider other detoxification services run in 'less specialised ways' which were not necessarily dealing with habitual drunkenness offenders, but with a wider range of persons with drinking problems who required detoxification. Following consultations between the Research Liaison Group, the DHSS and the research team, it was decided to continue the study of the Leeds and Manchester experimental centres but to widen the brief of the research project to include three additional detoxification centres as examples of other types of detoxification provision. The centres chosen by the DHSS were:

The Tower Hamlets detoxification centre
The Booth House detoxification centre was sited within the Booth House hostel, Whitechapel, in the East End of London, and was administered by the Salvation Army. It formed part of a network of facilities including an assessment centre in the East End and a 'dry hostel' in Swindon. It admitted only males.

The Oxford detoxification centre
Chilton Ward, Ley Clinic, Littlemore Hospital, Oxford, formed part of a complex with the Alcohol Treatment Unit. The ward was set aside solely for detoxification. Admissions were both male and female and there were no restrictions on sources of referral.

Portsmouth
DEP were also requested to study detoxification services within St James Hospital in Portsmouth, which – although it had an Alcohol Treatment Unit – had no specific setting for detoxification. Nevertheless, it was felt important to consider how detoxification

occurred in the day-to-day running of a psychiatric hospital's general admission wards.

2
Profiles of the Five Detoxification Centres

The following descriptions are of the centres as they were during the periods of study.

LEEDS: A COMMUNITY-BASED, DESIGNATED CENTRE

Introduction

The community-based Leeds Detoxification Centre was the first of the experimental centres to be opened. It opened in May 1976 and was funded by the DHSS for a three-year experimental period; central funding was then extended for a further six months. It formed part of the St Anne's Shelter and Housing Action, a well-established non-statutory agency serving the homeless, which also ran a day shelter, day support centre, three after-care hostels and two group homes. It was situated in St Mark's House, a large house about three-quarters of a mile from the centre of Leeds.

The centre had accommodation for over 20 men; besides the holding room (with beds for men to lie on until they had sobered up sufficiently), the centre proper had 20 beds, five of which were designated as 'after care' beds which were used both for men who had been referred to the detox from Scalebor Park, having been sent there for treatment from the detox, and by men who had completed the detox programme who were awaiting a place in one of the St Anne's Project houses. In addition, there was a lounge, a kitchen, bathroom facilities and staff offices. There was also a large garden at the back of the house which could be used by the men.

The staff of the Leeds Detox consisted of a director who was also director of St Anne's Shelter and Housing Action, a centre co-ordinator, six nurses (all of whom had the status of charge nurse), five care assistants, six social workers (one of whom was responsible for after-care work within the community) and a home care team made up of a housekeeper, cook and cleaners. The detox was also serviced by project administrative staff and a finance officer. The director and co-ordinator had responsibility for a wide range of activities and project personnel. Not the least of the director's duties was to ensure the future funding of the detox centre and other parts of St Anne's project.

19

Goals

> The centre has two main purposes:
> (a)   to provide a constructive alternative to the penal system for deal-
> ing with the person who is habitually arrested for offences of public
> drunkenness.
> (b)   to offer the homeless alcoholic the opportunity to escape from his
> present destructive life style.
> (The Detoxification Centre, St Mark's House, Leeds, 'How the
> Detoxification Centre Works', paragraph 1, p. 4, November 1978)

It should be noted that since the end of the experimental period,
during which the centre was studied, the detox developed and
broadened the services it provided; for example, it now admits
women and has increased in capacity by relocating the after-care unit
in one of the other project houses. It has also radically changed its
programme and the number of social work staff has been reduced
from six to three.

Referral

The centre only catered for homeless males referred by police. When
the centre first opened, only Millgarth Police Division, which covers
the inner city of Leeds, operated the referral system, and the detox
only accepted admissions between 2 p.m. and 8 p.m. After consultation with the staff and the police, the admission times were unre-
stricted, day or night. Moreover, two further police divisions,
Chapel Town and Ireland Wood, covering areas outside the inner
city, were included in the detox catchment area.

The criteria for referral operated by the police were that the client
be male, of no fixed abode and arrested within the detox catchment
area for being drunk and disorderly or drunk and incapable.

However, he would not be admitted if he was in urgent need of
medical or surgical attention, if he had also committed some other
offence, if he refused to be admitted to the detox, if the detox was full
or if he was banned from the detox. Clients making frequent re-
admissions were sometimes 'banned' temporarily by the detox staff,
because of the fear that they would have become dependent upon the
detox system. There were no formal procedures or set periods for
bans, but they never lasted longer than a month. Admission to the
centre was entirely voluntary. Men could leave at any time during the
programme.

Admission

Once a man passed through the entrance of the detox, the police role
was complete. Upon admission, a client was taken to the holding
room. The time spent in the holding room varied between one hour

and one day; in general, few clients spent more than 24 hours in the holding room. The policy of the centre was one of minimal use of drugs when drying out; during the drying-out process the client was 'talked down' by one of the care assistants or nurses. Some clients discharged themselves from the holding room, others were referred elsewhere for medical treatment while the remainder moved into the next stage of the programme.

Medical care

Although GPs were available on call throughout the 24 hours, in practice, GPs only needed to attend the detox three times a week. A client was examined at some stage during his first admission and thereafter at intervals of between three and six months if and when he reappeared in the centre, or if he required special attention. Naturally GPs were unable to see all new admissions since many left after only a brief stay. The consultant psychiatrist of the local Regional Alcoholism Treatment Unit (RATU) also attended the detox for a session a week to see clients who needed to be referred to psychiatric facilities and to advise the staff.

Social work programme

When a client moved on from the holding room, he started the rehabilitative phase of the 10-day programme.

Clients were encouraged to attend group counselling sessions and received individual, formal and informal counselling from their social worker. Counselling involved dealing with practical issues such as assistance with accommodation, employment and finance as well as advice on personal difficulties and how to cope with their drinking problem. Clients also received informal counselling from the nurse and care assistant.

Patient activities

The clients were expected to assist with domestic tasks, such as cleaning and making meals, and to participate generally in the running of the centre. They also were expected to participate generally in centre decision making.

Discharge and referral out

Decisions about discharge destinations were made collectively at the daily staff meeting. Clients were discharged to a range of places which could be classified into four different types: rooms or bedsits, accommodation where drinking was tolerated but where there was some supervision (e.g. Salvation Army hostel, DHSS reception centre, etc.), specialist facilities for the treatment and rehabilitation of alcoholics, ex-offenders, etc. (e.g. RATUs, St Anne's project

houses), and specialist facilities for the elderly and chronically infirm
(e.g. Social Services part II accommodation and long-term hospital
care).

The social worker of the project houses acted as a 'gatekeeper' for
the three rehabilitation houses and group homes. It is to him/her that
detox clients were formally referred. Criteria for entry to the house
centred around the stability of the resident group, the man's reputa-
tion, and his ability to mix with others.

Local agencies for problem drinkers and the single homeless

Leeds had a well-developed system of services for the single homeless
problem drinker. The majority were provided by the St Anne's
Housing Action Project.

There were seven rehabilitation hostels, a day support centre for
those living in these hostels or other forms of accommodation, a day
shelter and a night shelter. Both shelters provided medical care
amongst the other services.

There were three non-statutory, non-commercial common
lodging-houses and a statutory one. There was also a small hostel for
homeless women.

Outside the city there was a reception centre which concentrated
on resettlement. In the centre of the city there was a Homeless
Offenders Unit run by the probation service.

For the home based (and in some cases the homeless problem
drinkers), there was the council on alcoholism and some way out of
the city the Regional Alcoholism Treatment Unit.

Opportunities for more formal co-ordination and liaison were
provided by the Community Services Meeting to which representatives from agencies for problem drinkers and the single homeless
were invited.

MANCHESTER: A HOSPITAL-BASED, DESIGNATED CENTRE

Introduction

The Manchester detox, the second experimental centre set up as a
response to the 1971 Weiler Report, was opened in October 1977.
During the experimental period it was funded by the DHSS,
although the medical staff were provided by the regional health
authority. It was a purpose-built hospital ward adjoining the
psychiatric department at Withington Hospital. The hospital is four
miles from the Manchester city centre. Initially, patients could only
be referred by the police. However, because it was found that the
centre had been receiving insufficient admissions, the DHSS·decided

to permit the detox to take admissions from two other referral sources, namely, the Greater Manchester Council on Alcoholism (GMCA) and two hostels' GPs in July 1979.

The detox centre consisted of six 'Stage I' treatment cubicles, nine 'Stage II' beds (one four-bedded room; two two-bedded rooms; and one single room), a day room, dining room, a quiet room and various staff offices.

The staff of the detox were as follows: 1 consultant psychiatrist (shared with the Alcohol Treatment Unit (ATU)), 3 research registrars, 1 nursing officer (shared with ATU), 3 charge nurses, 1 staff nurse, 3 SENs, 6 nursing assistants, 1 community nurse, 5 clerks and two full-time social workers. When required, the detox had the services of a clinical psychologist and liaised with the Senior Registrar in Psychiatry primarily attached to the ATU.

Goals

The goals of the detox, as described by the staff in June 1980, were to provide homeless and home-based alcoholics and alcohol abusers with opportunities for detoxification, rehabilitation, education, assessment, medical and social work help and referral out. The detox was regarded as an alternative to the penal system for the habitual drunkenness offender. It aimed to contribute, through research, to a greater understanding of this group and to influence social policy makers.

Referrals

Originally, the police were asked to take anyone they had picked up for a simple drunkenness offence to the detox but the police decided to take them to the police station first; later this procedure was changed so that the officer apprehending the man or woman no longer needed to take them to the station prior to their admission to the detox. At first, the catchment area from which clients could be brought to the centre involved only the two police divisions covering South Manchester. This was soon extended to include a further two divisions, covering Stockport and Trafford. The six police catchment areas covered Manchester, Salford, Stockport and Trafford. In the last year of the experimental period, referrals were also accepted from the Greater Manchester Council on Alcoholism (GMCA) and the two GPs serving the Morning Star hostel.

Referrals could be male or female, and homeless or of fixed abode. The criteria for referral by the police were that the clients should be, or appear to be, drunkenness offenders; they should not be physically or mentally ill; they should not have committed any other criminal offence and not be wanted by the police for any previous offence; they should be willing to receive treatment.

The GMCA and GP referrals should be acutely intoxicated, likely to present withdrawal symptoms or be withdrawing and be requiring detoxification. If they had not previously been seen by a member of the centre staff, they would be seen on arrival to make sure that they thought that admission was justifiable. Clients from any referral source were refused admission if they were obviously mentally ill, severely physically injured or if they had taken a drug overdose, and therefore needed to be referred to another part of the hospital. Also, if the client had been admitted in the past and had a record of not benefitting from previous admissions, then the detox might ban them from readmittance for a set period, such as one month or six months.

The detox therefore allowed for direct access for police referrals but by arrangement only for other agencies' clients.

Admission

On arrival at the centre the client waited in the reception area where, if possible, the admissions clerk obtained details of his/her name, address, age, etc. The client was given a shower and deloused, if necessary, before being allocated to one of the Stage I cubicles. All the patients went into the Stage I cubicles for a minimum of 24 hours during which time their withdrawal symptoms were monitored and the doctor would see them daily (all the Stage I cubicles are covered by a closed-circuit TV system for observing patients). While in Stage I they were kept in their pyjamas; they were not confined to their cubicles, they could move about the Stage I and reception area but could not enter the Stage II area.

Medical care

There was always a doctor on duty to attend to the clinical needs of the patients. During the experimental period the doctor had a dual function of providing medical care and collecting research data. The doctor examined all patients and took blood for routine tests when they were admitted to the centre. During their stay in the centre they also had a chest X-ray. The patients' future plans were discussed and their discharge was decided by the staff at their daily meeting.

Social work programme

When clients were considered sufficiently physically improved they would move on to Stage II where they started attending discussion groups and participating in the normal functioning of the centre. The daily discussion groups were run by the nurses. These were informal but attendance was compulsory. The doctor also gave weekly informal lectures on the physical dangers of alcohol. Again, the clients were encouraged to bring up any thoughts or problems to do with their health. The nurses also saw the patients on a one-to-one basis to give advice and support. The social workers provided counselling and advice about drinking problems, finances, discharge places, or any other problems patients might have had. The social workers also liaised with the rehabilitation hostels in and around Manchester, and could try and place some of the clients in them.

The full detox programme took 10 days, the first day or two spent in Stage I and the remaining days spent in Stage II.

Patient activities

The patients were responsible for making their own beds, doing their personal laundry and washing up after meals on a rota system.

Discharge and referral out

There were a number of alternatives at discharge: patients could go to dry houses or hostels which might have been therapeutic or non-therapeutic; they could attend a short-term patient programme at the centre (usually for two weeks) travelling from home, a Salvation Army hostel, a local council hostel or from whatever accommodation had been arranged for them. They could go directly to the ATU in Withington Hospital or attend a day patient programme until there was a space in the ATU; they could discharge themselves requesting no further help or treatment. The social workers and the community nurse were responsible for trying to follow up and maintain contact with the clients that had been through the detox. The centre regarded it as important to maintain contact with clients and they were encouraged to visit whenever they wished. Patients could discharge themselves at any time and would be asked to leave if they drank alcohol while in the centre.

Local agencies for problem drinkers and single homeless

Greater Manchester had a wide range of facilities for single homeless and problem drinkers. Apart from the ATU at Withington Hospital, there was also another ATU at Prestwich Hospital. The GMCA ran a number of community-based clinics as well as the main counselling centre in the centre of Manchester.

There were seven rehabilitation hostels run by statutory and non-statutory agencies. Group homes were also provided by the local social services department.

There was a rehabilitation and reception centre run by the Supplementary Benefit Commission (SBC) at Walkden. There, too, was a probation service homeless and after-care unit.

Manchester and Salford both had large scale co-operation lodging-houses. There, too, were lodging-houses provided by non-statutory agencies with a Christian orientation.

The GMCA had a multi-facilities group which had representatives from agencies for problem drinkers and which acted as a co-ordination and liaison group.

OXFORD: A HOSPITAL-BASED CENTRE

Introduction

The detox was part of the Littlemore Hospital in Littlemore, a small village 3½ miles from the centre of Oxford. The detox had eight beds, was on the first floor of the Ley Clinic which ran a three-month treatment programme for alcoholics, both on an in-patient and day basis. The detox was set up in 1975, by the staff of the Ley Clinic, in an attempt to extend the system of services available to alcoholics and alcohol abusers. It was funded out of the area health general psychiatric budget.

The detox (in conjunction with the Ley Clinic) was staffed by a consultant psychiatrist, a clinical assistant and two full-time registrars on six-monthly rotation. The nursing staff was made up of three charge nurses, six staff nurses (one of whom is on nights at any given time). All were either registered mental nurses (RMNs) or state registered nurses (SRNs). The nursing staff worked in shifts so that there were at least two nurses on duty from 7 a.m. to 8.30 p.m. while a staff nurse with one night nurse covered the night period. The non-medical staff were made up of an occupational therapist, who took relaxation sessions with the detox patients, and one social worker/therapist (whose primary concern was follow-up and research on the treatment programme). There were often student nurses or trainee social workers or doctors on placement at the clinic.

Goals

The goal of the detox was to provide quick and easy access to facilities for drying out, assessment, medical care and referral for alcoholics in the region – and not only for those who were well motivated towards sobriety. The catchment area of the detox was the Oxford Regional Health Authority area.

Referrals

Referrals were accepted from all generic and specialist agencies. The most common were from GPs. Others might have come from probation officers, the Oxford Cyrenians, and councils on alcoholism. The referral system was designed on the assumption that the referring agent would have assessed the patient's need for detoxification. Where the referring agent was unknown to the clinic, the staff would ask the agent to accompany the patient to the clinic (when a bed was available) so that he/she might be escorted away if not thought by staff to be in need of their service.

The first contact with a clinic was usually by phone; the referring agent or patient themselves phoned the detox to see if a bed was available. All such enquiries were recorded in a referral book along with information about what the enquirer was told about availability. The number of contacts of this nature with the centre would depend on bed availability, with some patients making up to three or more such contacts with the centre. Sometimes when a bed had been offered to someone it was held beyond the specified time by which the patient was told to arrive. However, if the patient arrived after the bed had been taken up by someone else, the staff on duty had to turn him/her away. Access to the detox was therefore by arrangement only.

Admissions

On admission the patient was invited into the offices where administrative details were taken. The admitting nurse also asked patients for details about their background, recent drinking, present medication and medical history.

If the patient was new to the detox, he/she was informed of the rules and expectations of patients in the ward. (The 'rules' were written up on the information board by the patients' lounge). Patients were to stay in pyjamas, not to go downstairs to the Ley Clinic, not to take any alcohol or drugs, and to keep their own common rooms tidy. It was explained to patients that if they drank or left the premises (without permission), they would be discharged. It was expected that patients would stay for five to seven days, depending on their condition.

Medical care

Unless the condition required urgent treatment, patients were seen within one or two hours by one of the clinic doctors, were given a general medical check-up and any drugs required were prescribed. Few were given medication for withdrawal; it depended on the individual case. If it was found to be necessary, heminevrin was prescribed. Patients would then be seen and medical treatment reviewed routinely each morning (or more often if withdrawal was complicated by other factors). At this stage the doctors and nursing staff began to elicit any personal, family or social problems patients might have had and they were encouraged to discuss their problems with staff.

Social work support

There was no specific social worker attached to the detox. Patients were encouraged to be self-reliant, where possible, and help and support was available from the nurses and doctors.

Every patient coming into the detox was fully assessed. This assessment interview covered medical, psychological and social problems and attempted to build up a picture of the patient's life-style and attitudes. The assessment interview was also seen as a means to foster the relationship between staff and the patient and encourage motivation and insight.

Patient activities

Apart from keeping their own common rooms tidy, the patients were expected to help in any practical way those confined to bed, set tables, serve up meals and wash up after meals. There was a television in the patients' lounge. When not talking to staff and other patients, much of their time was spent watching television, listening to the radio, reading and resting on their beds.

Discharge and referral out

If patients left on their own initiative they would be asked to sign a self discharge form.

As one of the major aims was to ensure that patients leaving the detox had been given every opportunity of referral to treatment, they were all offered follow-up appointments as out-patients at the clinic or very occasionally in their own homes. This appointment was usually made by the person who assessed the patient and was recorded in the notes and copied on the discharge form.

The majority of patients returned to their own home address. Otherwise, no accommodation was specifically arranged for patients. They were informed about what was available, but it was left up to them to make necessary arrangements. Occasionally, it might be thought appropriate for the patient to be referred to a psychiatric service or to some type of intermediate care such as referral to a liver clinic, epilepsy clinic or the social services.

Local agencies for problem drinkers and the single homeless

Oxford had a limited number of facilities for the single homeless and problem drinkers.

There were two rehabilitation hostels for alcoholics run by the local council on alcoholism in conjunction with the Ley Clinic. They took both men and women.

In addition, there was the Ley Community which was a long-term rehabilitation facility for ex-drug abusers, alcoholics and young offenders.

There were two non-statutory facilities for the single homeless. One provided a day and night shelter for both men and women and the other provided residential facilities.

There was a probation day centre to which problem drinkers

could go. Otherwise there was a guest house which took people discharged from the Ley Clinic.

The Oxford and District Council on Alcoholism had paid staff and has representatives on it from the Ley Clinic.

TOWER HAMLETS: A COMMUNITY-BASED CENTRE

Introduction

The Tower Hamlets Detoxification Centre was opened in September 1975. It formed a small part of a sizeable complex run by the Salvation Army in the Tower Hamlets district of London. The Tower Hamlets detox was situated in the basement of Booth House, a hostel for working men, with a bail wing for first-time offenders and part III accommodation for elderly men. Adjoining this was the Victoria Home, a common lodging-house for vagrants.

It was funded, in part, by the DHSS, the Salvation Army and through contributions from residents' SBC payments.

The detox centre consisted of sleeping accommodation for nine (one bedroom for six, and three single rooms), a medical room, baths, toilets, a kitchen/dining room and day room. There were also three offices and a staff room.

The centre was staffed by a warden (who was also a nurse), a social worker, five care assistants, a secretary and a domestic. The warden did a six-day week and was on call most nights. The social worker and secretary both worked a normal five-day week but the social worker worked into the evening if necessary. The care assistants worked shifts of 7.30 a.m. to 3.30 p.m. and 2.45 p.m. to 10.45 p.m. Except during periods of overlap, there was usually only one on duty, although occasionally a third shift of 9 a.m. to 5 p.m. was added. There was a care assistant on call every night in a flat by the men's sleeping quarters. The staffing as described was somewhat unusual in that one of the care assistants had been taken on temporarily to cover the holiday period and it was planned that another, who was a SEN, would take over some of the nurses' duties from the warden once she was established.

Goals

The goal of the detox was to provide a contact point and initial treatment centre for alcoholics, and in particular, to give help with medical, social and psychological problems.

Referrals

There were no formal arrangements with any agency concerning referrals; the centre did not function in co-ordination with the police to provide an alternative to prison for drunkenness offenders. Entry to the centre was completely voluntary. Self-referrals were the most common source of referrals; the other sources were social workers, probation officers, courts, Salvation Army hostels, hospitals or doctors, family or friends of clients, and other centres. Referrals could be made by phone or in person at the centre; however, the decision to admit a man was made only when the applicant had been seen in person by the warden or social worker (or in a few cases, if neither were available, by a care assistant).

Admission was not automatic, but more than half the referrals made since the centre opened in 1975 resulted in the client being admitted to the centre. Of those who were not admitted to the centre a few were referred elsewhere, a few were invited to return at a later date and almost half did not turn up at the centre.

The centre only took men, but they could be either homeless or of fixed abode. All applicants must have attended an interview before being admitted, so that the warden, social worker or care assistant could assess his physical condition and his 'motivation'. There were various criteria for admission. A client must have been in true need of detoxification (i.e. he must have consumed alcohol within the last 48 hours or be having acute delayed withdrawal symptoms). Men who had only briefly broken their period of sobriety did not qualify for admission, i.e. a man who had been drinking for a day or two after his release from prison or discharge from hospital would not qualify for admission. Anyone who was felt to be misusing the centre for shelter rather than detoxification would not be admitted. If a client was in need of specialist medical help he would be referred to a hospital rather than admitted to the detox. The centre also would not accept applicants who were in a 'condition of residence' or who were due to appear in court within the next seven days. When the detox had more applicants than places available, it aimed to take the most highly motivated clients (this was assessed by considering a client's previous record with the centre and any other recent treatment he had received). Applicants arriving when the centre was full were given a preliminary interview and may have been asked to return at a later date; applicants applying by phone were asked to try again when a vacancy was due. Times of admission were limited; no one was seen with a view to admission after 10.30 p.m. and before 7.30 a.m. If a man came to the centre asking to be admitted between those hours, he would be asked to return the following morning.

Access to the detox was therefore by arrangement only; there was no equivalent procedure for direct admission of referrals as there was at designated centres.

Although there was no set policy on the number of readmissions, a man was unlikely to be readmitted within three months of his previous admission. This period might have been longer or shorter depending on the man, his efforts, and the number of beds available. There was a low incidence of heavy repeaters since the opening of the centre; the maximum number of admissions made by any one person was six. There was also no banning procedure.

The detox had no defined catchment area.

Admission

On admission clients had a bath and a preliminary medical examination before being put to bed where they were kept for 24–36 hours. All clients were prescribed vitamins, and some may have been prescribed tranquillisers and sleeping tablets. Infestation was rare; there were about half a dozen cases in five years. The centre provided the men with pyjamas and their personal possessions were locked away for them. Any money they had was counted and put in the safe after having deducted their contribution towards board and lodgings. The amount to be contributed towards board and lodging was discussed and agreed at their admission interview. A man could not claim benefit, supplementary or unemployment, while he was in the centre because he was not allowed out of the centre to sign on. The centre, however, could claim for the cost of the man's up-keep if the man had not received any money (and had less than £5 on him) for a week prior to admission, but the DHSS would only pay a maximum of three nights' allowance for each man even if his stay exceeded a week.

Whether in bed or not, the men were kept in their pyjamas during their stay in the centre; this was a means to ensure that they did not go out and begin drinking.

Medical care

The centre was always covered by nursing staff, either by the warden when she was on duty or on call, or by one of the other nurses who worked for Booth House and Victoria Home. There were also two visiting doctors, one who came on Sunday mornings and one who came on Wednesday afternoons. Thus, every client who stayed at least three days should have been given a full medical check-up.

Social work support

Each client was interviewed by the social worker on about the third day of his stay, or when he was sufficiently physically improved to be up and about. The social worker asked for personal details, including details relating to his drinking problem, and discussed with him whatever practical help he might need, such as help in finding accommodation or further treatment. There was no group therapy because it was felt that there was insufficient time for a group to establish itself due to the almost constant turnover of men. Very occasionally the social worker might have held a group meeting in which he discussed the various facilities and treatment available and encouraged the men to speak of their own experiences of these facilities. Similarly, the warden might have given an occasional lecture on the physical effects of alcoholism but neither of these group activities were standard practice. The social worker also tried to see every man in the centre for a few minutes on Friday as he was only available on some weekends. When the social worker was absent, all his duties were taken on by the warden.

The full detox programme was intended to run for seven days. However, many men discharged themselves, and one or two were discharged by the staff, before this period had elapsed; the length of stay might also have been extended beyond seven days.

Patient activities

The residents were expected to do light chores which were assigned to them by the assistants: they made their own beds, did some sweeping and cleaning, made tea and snacks (main meals were brought down from the hostel kitchens upstairs), took meals to those in bed and washed up. In their spare time they could watch TV, read books, play games, listen to the radio or records. Their day was very structured: the times they got up, went to bed, had their meals and morning and afternoon tea were all set out. They also had to attend daily prayers.

Discharge and referral out

A resident could discharge himself at any time and could be discharged by the staff if it was felt that he was disruptive. In the normal course of events, after seven days the clients were discharged with a letter from the social worker to take to the DHSS stating that they had been receiving treatment at the centre and outlining their future plans. Some clients had prior arrangements to move on to a treatment unit after they had been dried out at the detox. However, if they had no such arrangements but required further treatment, the detox had a formal arrangement with the local assessment unit, also run by the Salvation Army, whereby its warden or another member of staff visited the detox weekly to interview prospective clients. About 40 per cent of the admissions were referred out to Salvation Army institutions whether they were hostels or treatment units. Referrals were also made to non-Salvation Army units. There was no formal follow-up as such, but there may have been feedback from other agencies.

Local agencies for problem drinkers and the single homeless

The London Borough of Tower Hamlets had a range of facilities in fairly close proximity to each other and which included day and residential provision.

There were three day and evening centres for the single homeless (one of which was just outside Tower Hamlets in the City). These provided advice and counselling and could refer clients to the centre. There were three rehabilitation hostels for problem drinkers which varied in certain specific ways. The Salvation Army Assessment Unit and B Sharp ran short-term treatment programmes, while the third hostel only provided for those with TB. B Sharp also had four long-stay houses. All these facilities were for men only.

There were a number of large-scale lodging-houses run by charitable agencies, four of which were run by the Salvation Army and two by local church organisations.

Otherwise there was a range of cheap high- and low-grade commercial lodging-houses in the area.

No Fixed Abode was the co-ordinating agency for Tower Hamlets and had as its members all the non-commercial, non-statutory organisations for single homeless and problem drinkers.

PORTSMOUTH: A NON-SPECIALIST, HOSPITAL-BASED SERVICE

Introduction

Unlike the four other centres, St James Hospital did not have a centre or ward specifically for the purpose of detoxification.

St James Hospital was situated just outside the centre of Portsmouth, in extensive grounds rather more typical of mental hospitals in rural areas. It had approximately 500 beds which serviced a catchment area of approximately 323,000 people. This area was split into five patient populations of approximately 60,000 to 70,000 each, the boundaries of which were consistent with local social services areas.

There were three wards at St James Hospital where patients were admitted for detoxification: Solent (32 beds), King Villa (36 beds) and Pink Villa (22 beds). Nelson Ward, set apart from the main hospital but within its grounds, was an Alcoholism Treatment Unit with 9 beds for men and 3 for women. Occasionally beds would be used for drying out patients who had been accepted onto the treatment programme.

Each general ward had one or two consultants, one or two registrars, a duty doctor and nursing staff made up of at least three trained staff and several student nurses (who stayed between 8 and 12 weeks). The consultants held a case conference once a week on their own patients and were available to their ward staff and patients two to three times a week.

Referral

When referrals for detoxification were made, the general ward allocated for this purpose was dictated by the catchment area from which the patient came. Solent Ward required referrals to come via a GP while the other two took directly from a range of sources. The most common were as follows: GP, social workers, the hospital out-patient department, Havant Day Hospital, general hospitals and non-statutory agencies (e.g. Hampshire Council on Alcoholism). Police referrals were generally refused by Solent and King Villa, because it was assumed the person had low motivation. Self referrals were most likely to be accepted by Pink Villa. Referrals were accepted by all three wards when made by hospital personnel specialising in alcoholism.

Admission

On admission to a ward the nurse opened a temporary admission folder. A physical examination was given, which included neurological tests, blood counts and tests for liver damage; and X-rays were done to detect any chest trouble and for head injuries should the person have had a recent fall, etc. The doctor then noted what medication was to be used and this, together with the results of the tests, formed part of a daily record kept of the patients' progress. A nurse informed the medical record department as well as other appropriate departments of the admission.

Once examined, patients were usually given a bath and talked to about their reasons for coming to the ward. Their belongings were checked for alcohol or pills. Any drugs were removed and patients were warned about the no drinking rule. Solent ward discharged patients who were found drinking while King Villa and Pink Villa often allowed them to stay, after a warning. Once settled patients were introduced to the ward routine and to other patients. They were not required to change into pyjamas.

Medical care

The kinds of medication given varied for the different wards. In Solent Ward patients were taken off Valium but other drugs were administered by nursing staff if the patient was already being treated by a GP. In the other wards no drugs were administered apart from those required to assist the drying-out process. The Solent Ward and

Pink Villa used Chlormethiazole (Heminevrin) on a reducing dose for seven days, and a course of strong vitamin injections for the same period. King Villa had a policy of using Librium or Valium, 10 mg two to three times a day, and also provided vitamin injections and sleeping pills if required. In all wards a Valium injection was given if the patient had a fit. Weight charts were kept if the patient was under-nourished and extra vitamins were given, e.g. Thiamine.

Social work and therapy

A medical social worker attended the ward case conference and would follow up the patients after discharge, if necessary. There was a community nurse available to provide follow-up if a patient was referred on to the Havant Day Hospital. The social workers were described as mainly dealing with patients' financial and accommodation problems. These services appeared particularly relevant to Pink Villa as the staff said that approximately one-third of their patients were of no fixed abode while the other two wards were thought to have home-based patients.

All patients had to go to occupational therapy every day, which included some group therapy. In these groups detox patients were mixed with other types of patients. Whether this mix was appropriate was the subject of some debate amongst staff as they found that detox and other patients did not easily identify with each others' problems.

Group meetings were also held in each of the wards on either a daily or weekly basis to discuss any problems patients might have.

AA meetings are not held in the hospital. They used to be, but it was found that patients felt obliged to attend as they understood this to be a compulsory part of the treatment (particularly those in Nelson Ward). Hence, it was decided to hold meetings outside the hospital so that patients might attend on a voluntary basis.

Patient activities

While on the ward patients were expected to change their own sheets, wash their clothing, make their beds, and participate in the rota for washing up after meals and laying tables. All food was prepared centrally and delivered. Patients could make tea and coffee any time they wished. During occupational therapy (and outside group therapy) the mornings were taken up with activities such as basket making, art and woodwork. In the afternoon there were cards and games and some relaxation exercises. For the evenings, back in the ward, there were records, a piano, television and table tennis.

Discharge and referral out

Patients could leave at any time. The decision to discharge a patient was the responsibility of the consultant, although all staff were consulted. Patients were referred to the Nelson Ward, if they expressed the desire for treatment, but only a small proportion did.

Patients referred from the three wards to Nelson Ward were likely to encounter a waiting list of between two and eight weeks. Those who were homeless were taken up in sequence and no special arrangements were made to find accommodation for them during this period. However, it was thought that this did not prejudice their chances of treatment as few homeless people appeared to drop out between first contact for referral and ultimate admission to the centre.

Those who came to Nelson Ward in need of drying out (and without going through any of the other wards) were not expected to participate in the six-week programme for two weeks as it was felt that they needed time to adjust. The ATU required strict adherence to a no-drink rule, which – if broken – was met with discharge.

Once having left, patients were able to attend the out-patients clinic and/or groups run by the ATU for ex-patients. They might have attended a family group run by the marriage guidance counsellor. There were no after-care facilities attached to the hospital for problem drinkers.

Local agencies for problem drinkers and the single homeless

Portsmouth had no rehabilitation hostels for problem drinkers. The nearest were those provided by St Dismas in Southampton.

The Portsmouth Housing Association, in partnership with St James Hospital, had short- and long-term accommodation for ex-mental patients. This accommodation was managed by the community nursing officer at St James. Long-term accommodation in the form of bedsits was provided by a non-statutory organisation, HACRO (Hampshire Association for the Care and Resettlement of Offenders) in conjunction with the probation service. The bedsits could accommodate men and women who were stable problem drinkers. Of a similar grade of housing was the lodging-house run for ex-navy men which would take alcoholics if well behaved.

There were two non-statutory agencies that provided for the chronic single homeless, one of which had a soup run. Both would take problem drinkers. Another project provided a first-stage house for the chronic single homeless and the opportunity to move on to their second and third-stage accommodation. The third stage was independent, long-term accommodation.

Otherwise, Portsmouth had a range of cheap board and lodgings and bed and breakfast accommodation as well as various commercial lodging-houses which provided cheap and substandard accommodation. The availability of this accommodation varied according to the season.

3
The Process of Detoxification

INTRODUCTION

The question of the extent and severity of withdrawal symptoms manifested by clients admitted to the detoxification centre is considered in this chapter along with the different treatment programmes operated in each of the centres.

One of the assumptions in the Weiler Report was that the target population, namely habitual drunkenness offenders, would comprise heavy drinkers/problem drinkers likely to have serious withdrawal problems and probably to be in need of medical care. This assumption formed the basis of many of the recommendations for the type of facility that would be required in terms of the experience, number and type of staff required; the type of facility required – specialist versus non-specialist; and the degree of sophistication of 'medical' equipment required, etc.

In describing the processes adopted in each centre, the 'comparability' of the different centres can be clarified. For the purposes of comparing and contrasting the centres a degree of uniformity, across the centres, is necessary. Nevertheless, the differences are of paramount importance since these give an insight into the different effects that can be achieved by different services, and the different demands for which centres might be required to cater. The more practical questions about the day-to-day running of the centres were explored.

The differences between the centres, as outlined in the profiles (chapter 2) were strongly reflected in the procedures followed at each centre. It was necessary, therefore, to study the various stages of the process of detoxification at each centre, namely:
Admission
Residence in detoxification centres
Practical help and emotional support
Patient activities
Discharge and referral out
Procedures adopted by the five centres with regard to clients referred, the drug regimes, etc. were monitored at each of the centres over a set period of time.

It is interesting to note that while all but the general psychiatric hospital in Portsmouth called themselves detoxification centres, the

38

procedures they adopted and the clients they catered for were very different. Those referred to the designated centres by the police tended to manifest a broader range of problems, not just health related, and as such were in need of practical and emotional support. Their problems were chronic. This was also the case for the Salvation Army Hostel in Tower Hamlets. In contrast, patients admitted to the centre in Oxford had problems which were generally more acute in nature. To some extent this was reflected in the administration of drugs although there were other factors (such as staffing levels) that may have influenced the frequency with which drugs were or were not administered. The differences in types of clients was again linked with the types of after-care facilities that were used or with which the detoxes had contact.

ADMISSION

Leeds

Referrals at the Leeds centre were only supposed to come from police. The criteria for referral are outlined in the centre profiles in chapter 2. During the monitoring period, no self-referrals or referrals from anywhere other than the police were admitted to the Leeds Detoxification Centre.

Once a man passed through the entrance to the centre, the police role was complete. Upon admission, all clients were taken into a reception room, the 'Holding Room', just to the left of the entrance. Here they remained until they were sober or well enough to enter the unit proper, unless they decided in the meantime to leave the centre.

As a man entered the detoxification centre, the nurse or care assistant assessed his degree of intoxification and any signs of abuse of any other substances besides alcohol. The nurses also treated any minor cuts or injuries.

The policy of the Leeds centre was to 'talk down' intoxicated men, and not to use pharmacological aids. In most cases, intoxicated men eventually fell asleep on one of the divans in the holding room.

The initial stage of detoxification was relatively simple in terms of facilities, materials and medication, but fairly demanding for the staff, especially the nurses and care assistants, who were required to provide intoxified men with emotional support and attention for considerable periods of time.

Manchester

Referrals came from the police, the local council on alcoholism and two GPs serving the Morning Star hostel for those of no fixed abode. Referrals from the latter two were required to be acutely intoxicated.

On arrival at the centre clients waited in the reception area, where, if possible, the admissions clerk obtained details of their names, addresses, age, etc. Clients were given a shower and deloused if necessary, before being allocated to one of the Stage I cubicles. All the patients went into the Stage I cubicles for a minimum of 24 hours during which time their withdrawal symptoms were monitored. A doctor examined all patients and took blood samples for routine tests when they were admitted to the centre.

Tower Hamlets

At this centre there were no formal arrangements with any agency concerning referrals and although it dealt only with males, including many who were of no fixed abode, the centre did not function in co-ordination with the police to provide an alternative to prison for drunkenness offenders. Clients were interviewed and assessed for suitability prior to admission.

Applicants arriving when the centre was full were given a preliminary interview and, if accepted for admission, they would have been asked to return at a later date; applicants applying by phone were asked to try again when a vacancy was due. Times for admission were limited: no one was seen with a view to admission after 10.30 p.m. and before 7.30 a.m. If a man came to the centre asking to be admitted between these hours he was asked to return the following morning.

On admission, clients had a bath and a preliminary medical check before being put to bed where they were kept for 24–36 hours. All clients were prescribed vitamins, and the majority were administered with minor tranquillisers and sleeping tablets. The centre provided men with pyjamas and their personal possessions were kept locked away. Any money they had was counted and put in the safe, after discussion about how much the client could afford to pay for his stay.

Oxford

Unlike Tower Hamlets, the goal of the Oxford Detoxification Centre was to provide quick and easy access to facilities for drying out, assessment, medical care and referral for problem drinkers without any discrimination in favour of those who were well motivated towards sobriety.

Referrals were accepted from all generic and specialist agencies, including GPs, probation officers, the Oxford Cyrenians and councils on alcoholism. General practitioners were the most common referral source. It was assumed that the referring agent would have assessed the patient's need for detoxification. Where referral agents were unknown to the centre, they were asked to accompany the patient to the centre (when a bed was available) so that he/she could be escorted away if not thought by staff to be in need of their service.

On admission, the patient was invited into the offices where administrative details were taken. The admitting nurse also asked patients for details about their background, recent drinking, present medication and medical history.

If the patient was new to the detoxification centre, he/she was informed of the rules and expectations of patients in the ward. (The 'rules' were written up on the information board near the patients' lounge.) Patients stayed in pyjamas, were not to go downstairs to the Alcohol Treatment Unit, to take any alcohol or drugs, and were expected to keep their own rooms tidy. It was explained to the patients that if they drank or left the premises (wihout permission) they would be discharged.

Unless requiring urgent treatment, the patient was seen after one to two hours by one of the clinic doctors and given a medical check-up, and any necessary drugs were prescribed, usually Heminevrin.

Portsmouth

Unlike the four other centres, St James Hospital did not have a centre or ward specifically for the purpose of detoxification, but there were three general admission wards and an Alcohol Treatment Unit into which patients might be admitted for detoxification.

When referrals specifically for detoxification were made, the general ward to which they were allocated depended on the catchment area from which the patient came. One ward required referrals to come via GPs, while the other two took referrals directly from a range of sources, the most common being GPs, social workers, the hospital out-patient department, a local day hospital, general hospitals, and non-statutory agencies (e.g. Hampshire Council on Alcoholism). Police referrals were generally refused in two of the wards, because it was assumed such clients would have 'low motivation', but this was not stressed so much in the other general ward. Self-referrals were most likely to be accepted by this same ward where again it was assumed that motivation was not as important, when the primary need was for detoxification. Referrals were also accepted by all three wards when made by hospital personnel specialising in alcoholism.

On admission to a ward, a nurse opened a temporary admission folder. A physical examination was conducted, including neurological tests, blood counts, tests for liver damage, and any X-rays thought necessary, e.g. for chest disease. A doctor would then note what medication was to be used. A nurse informed the medical record department and any other appropriate departments of the admission. Once examined, the patients were expected to be bathed and talked to about their reasons for coming to the ward. Their belongings were checked for alcohol or pills. Any drugs were removed and the patients were warned about the no drinking rule. Once settled, they were introduced to the ward routine and to other patients. The patients were not required to change into pyjamas.

Admission procedures and clients' state upon admission

Information relating to the condition of clients upon admission was collected, such as, whether clients were in a state of drunkenness, withdrawal or had a simple hangover, or if they exhibited indications of other types of problems and whether medical or some other type of assistance was provided in the first six hours after admission. This was collected at each centre for a defined time period: namely nine weeks in Leeds and twelve weeks in each of the other centres. Despite this the average number of admissions per week, during these periods, was highest at Leeds (see table 3.1). In fact the average number of admissions per week at Tower Hamlets was exactly half that at Leeds despite the differences in the lengths of the study periods. Part of this was a function of repeating since no client admitted during the monitoring period was readmitted during the 12-week study in Tower Hamlets. However, at Leeds, all referrals were brought by the police and centre staff could only occasionally affect the general admission trends. Thus a quarter of the clients admitted during the nine weeks were admitted twice and seven (8 per cent) more than twice. At Manchester and Oxford, relatively little impression was made on the overall figures by clients repeating since only 13 per cent of Manchester admissions and 6 per cent at Oxford were repeats.

Times of admissions

At Leeds, over three-quarters (115, 79 per cent) of the admissions to the centre were made between 2 p.m. and midnight, the busiest period being the three hours before midnight, during which one in three admissions occurred.

At Manchester, admissions were fairly evenly distributed, with a third of admissions occurring in the afternoon, just over a quarter between midnight and 8 a.m. and the rest spread evenly over the remaining periods. However, this masked the different patterns exhibited by the police referrals and referrals from other sources. As at Leeds, fewer clients were brought by the police between 8 a.m. and 2 p.m. while the majority (79 per cent) of admissions were made between 2 p.m. and midnight. However, the police in Manchester were more likely to bring offenders in the small hours with one in three police referrals to Manchester arriving between midnight and

Table 3.1 Admissions during the monitoring period

	Leeds (9 weeks)	Manchester (12 weeks)	Tower Hamlets (12 weeks)	Oxford (12 weeks)	Portsmouth (12 weeks)
No. of admissions during the monitoring period	146	142	89	124	68*
No. resident during the monitoring period	146	157	97	124	68
Average no. of admissions per week	16.2	11.8	7.4	10.3	5.7

*Patients with a possible alcohol problem as suggested by the screening study

Table 3.2   Distribution of admission over time – per cent of admissions

Times of admission	Leeds	Manchester	Tower Hamlets	Oxford	Portsmouth
00.01–08.00	12	27	13	1	3
08.01–14.00	10	15	85	48	48
14.01–18.00	26	35	1	37	28
18.01–21.00	21	11	0	14	15
21.01–24.00	32	13	0	0	1
Not completed	–	1	–	–	4

8 a.m. Of the other referrals (i.e. non-police) to Manchester, 18 per cent arrived during these hours, but over three-quarters arrived in normal working hours, between 8 a.m. and 6 p.m. compared with only 30 per cent of police referrals. This demonstrated how the routine of a detoxification unit would necessarily vary according to whether it received police referrals or 'planned' admissions.

As explained, the Tower Hamlets admission procedures disallowed admissions after 10.30 p.m., but in fact only one client was found to be admitted after 2 p.m. during the monitoring period. Thus virtually all admissions occurred between 7.30 a.m. and 2.00 p.m.

Nearly half the Oxford admissions occurred during this same period, but a further third were made between 2 p.m. and 6 p.m. and 14 per cent between 6 p.m. and 9 p.m. Only one client was admitted during the monitoring period between 9 p.m. and 8 a.m. Virtually the same pattern pertained overall at Portsmouth as at Oxford, although, interestingly, the only four people admitted to general wards in Portsmouth between midnight and 8 a.m. during the monitoring period were identified as probably having drink problems (see table 3.2).

Clients' state on admission

Virtually every client at Leeds, in the opinion of the admitting nurses, was considered to be drunk upon admission. Only two (1 per cent) were considered to be withdrawing upon admission.

At the other three specialist detoxification centres (see table 3.3) it was predictably the other designated centre, Manchester, which came nearest to Leeds in admitting people in a drunken state. Two-thirds of their cases were recorded as such, but of the 20 per cent

Table 3.3 Clients' state on admission

	Leeds		Manchester		Tower Hamlets		Oxford		Portsmouth	
	No.	%	No.	%	No.	%	No.	%	No.	%
Drunk*	139	95	94	66	34	38	61	49	7	11
Withdrawing*	2	1	16	11	51	57	33	27	15	24
Hungover*	0	0	14	10	45	51	8	6	8	13
Sober*	0	0	28	20	44	49	35	28	21	33

*These categories are not mutually exclusive

recorded as sober upon admission 11 per cent were considered to be in a withdrawal state upon admission. Clearly there were differences according to the source of referral, with the police referrals being in a somewhat similar state to those at Leeds; 80 per cent were recorded as being drunk, compared to only half of those from the GMCA. Six per cent of Manchester police referrals were recorded as being in withdrawal upon admission, compared to 20 per cent of GMCA referrals, a finding which proved typical of unplanned police referrals as compared to the state of patients whose arrival had been arranged. Despite the referral system at Oxford, half the clients were drunk upon admission, compared to a quarter sober, and the others were thought to be withdrawing. The effect of the delayed admission procedure at Tower Hamlets also produced a recording of 49 per cent clients sober at admission, with over half thought to be withdrawing, compared to 38 per cent drunk.

At Portsmouth, virtually exactly the opposite picture pertained overall compared to Leeds, with most patients considered by their admitting nurse to be sober upon admission. Of course, at Portsmouth most clients were not expected to have a drink problem, yet even here 15 patients (24 per cent) were thought to be in a withdrawal state upon admission. Twelve of these were admitted not into the Alcohol Treatment Unit but into the general wards. Eight of these 12 were indicated by the screening tests to have drink problems, as were seven of the eight patients admitted drunk and all those eight admitted with a hangover. Possibly the four patients thought to be withdrawing but not indicated by the screening as problem drinkers might have been withdrawing from other drugs.

Besides classifying the clients' state within this general terminology, the nurses were asked to state on the admission form whether clients exhibited any of the following six indicators of a withdrawal state upon admission:
1   profuse sweating
2   fits and convulsions
3   marked hand tremor
4   marked body tremor
5   visual hallucinations
6   auditory hallucinations
None of the clients at Leeds displayed more than one of the six indicators of withdrawal. Clearly none of the Leeds clients could be considered to have been in a severe withdrawal state at this stage.

A similar picture emerged at Manchester, the other designated centre, but there was a slightly higher incidence of symptoms. However, at Tower Hamlets and Oxford, the clients exhibited indicators of withdrawal with a much greater frequency. This is not consistent with the finding that clients at these two centres were not drunk upon admission as often as clients at the designated centres.

However, it could be the case that as a result of the length of time between contacting the centre and subsequent admission, the clients of Tower Hamlets and Oxford had in many cases sobered up and advanced into a withdrawal state (see table 3.4). The data from Portsmouth was of a less concise nature since it referred to all patients entering a general psychiatric hospital. There was a higher incidence of visual and auditory hallucinations which may have had nothing to do with the effects of alcohol. Indeed the results of the screening study would indicate this, since it can be seen that most of those exhibiting sweating and hand and body shakes were indicated as problem drinkers, whereas only a small number of those recorded as hallucinating were found to have had a drink problem.

The proportion of clients who arrived in a confused and disorientated state was higher at all the special detoxification centres than at Portsmouth. Nevertheless at least three-quarters of clients at all centres were considered to be compliant and co-operative upon admission, even in 85 per cent of Leed's cases and 73 per cent at Manchester, to which clients had been brought by the police. However, the centre which reported the highest incidence of verbal aggression (12 per cent) and physical aggression (3 per cent) was Leeds, which may be a product of Leeds having been the only centre with an avowed policy of avoiding the use of all pharmacological aids.

Virtually no clients at any of the centres presented acute physical problems upon admission. Even vomiting and dry retching which might be thought common amongst clients upon admission to detoxification centres, in practice occurred only occasionally. Only five clients at Leeds (3 per cent) vomited, two at Manchester, three at Oxford and one at Portsmouth. No clients at all vomited during the initial admission period to Tower Hamlets, and only one case was reported there of dry retching compared to five (3 per cent) at Leeds, six (4 per cent) at Manchester, four (3 per cent) at Oxford and none at all at Portsmouth.

There were only five Leeds cases (3 per cent) which required treatment for injuries upon admission, two of whom could not be dealt with in the detoxification centre. Only six (4 per cent) required other medical assistance. No clients at any of the other centres required any of these things, apart from four (3 per cent) at Oxford who needed treatment for injuries, all of whom were able to be dealt with within the detoxification centre itself, and six (8 per cent) at Portsmouth who were all treated within the hospital.

Interestingly, the incidence of clients being infested upon admis-

Table 3.4 Clients' withdrawal symptoms on admission

Withdrawal symptom	Leeds		Manchester		Tower Hamlets		Oxford		Portsmouth	
	No.	%	No.	%	No.	%	No.	%	No.	%
Profuse sweating	6	4	16	11	25	28	25	20	12	18
Fits/convulsions	1	1	1	1	0	0	0	0	0	0
Marked hand tremor	8	6	12	8	32	36	32	26	22	32
Marked body tremor	0	0	5	4	10	11	12	10	6	9
Visual hallucinations	0	0	4	3	3	3	2	2	2	3
Auditory hallucinations	0	0	2	1	3	3	1	1	1	1

sion to the detoxification centres was very low. It was in fact only recorded in two cases at Tower Hamlets and one case at Portsmouth, but never at Leeds or Oxford. These four centres accounted for a total of over 500 monitored admissions. However, at Manchester 46 clients were recorded as being deloused soon after their admission. Moreover, 15 of them were not police referrals. However, they all appear to have been of no fixed abode. This should not be interpreted as defaming other facilities for the homeless in general in Manchester, since amongst a population who circulate between many institutions and sleeping quarters, it only takes one or two below-standard places to create a relatively wide incidence of infestation.

It is perhaps curious in this context that there should have been only two cases at Tower Hamlets who required delousing, when the East End of London was considered by some workers in the field to contain some of the most classical 'Skid Row' type drinkers in Britain. Yet the staff at Tower Hamlets reported only dealing with a few cases of infestation in their entire five years of operation. It may be that infestation was not as common there as in Manchester, or that the out-and-out Skid Row drinker in the East End was unlikely to be admitted to the Tower Hamlets detoxification centre. Moreover it should be noted that a previous study, by one of the nurses at Leeds of the first 100 admissions, found 5 per cent of clients to be infested upon admission. In this later study in Leeds there was no evidence of infestations even though the later sample included some of the men who had been included in the former study. It may be that a detoxification centre can help in 'cleaning up' a homeless population.

There were a few cases of clients exhibiting other skin disorders. There were also a few clients exhibiting evidence of either having overdosed on drugs other than alcohol and/or long-term drug abuse. The abuse of other substances besides alcohol appeared to be relatively uncommon among the detoxification centres studied during the monitoring period.

A major difference between centres emerged on the question of clients being recorded as having a permanent disability of any kind. Surprisingly, this was recorded in only two cases at Manchester, three at Tower Hamlets, five at Portsmouth and seven (6 per cent) at Oxford, but in 34 clients (23 per cent) at Leeds. This complies with other evidence that Leeds possibly had the most generally socially and physically disadvantaged of the five client populations.

Treatment received within the first six hours of admission

Virtually all entrants to the two hospital-based specialist detoxification centres at Manchester and Oxford were seen by a doctor within the first six hours of admission, but this never happened

Table 3.5 Drugs prescribed within first six hours of admission

	Leeds		Manchester		Tower Hamlets		Oxford		Portsmouth	
	No.	%	No.	%	No.	%	No.	%	No.	%
Sleeping tablets	1	1	3	2	84	94	0	0	5	7
Minor tranquillisers* (including valium, librium and similar drugs)	1	1	20	14	82	92	5	4	5	7
Major tranquillisers* (including Heminevrin and similar drugs)	0	0	35	25	7	8	86	69	33	49
Pain killers*	0	0	2	1	2	2	1	1	1	1

*These categories are not exclusive

at the community-based centres which relied on visiting doctor cover. The incidence of prescriptions of various drugs within the clients first six hours of admission also showed marked differences across the centres (see table 3.5). It is impossible to know the extent to which the differences were due to variations in prescription policies rather than the psychological states of individual clients at the different centres. Nevertheless the differences, particularly between Leeds and Oxford, were extreme. At Leeds, only one client received sleeping tablets and another minor tranquillisers. These were the only clients out of 146 monitored admissions to be prescribed any drugs within their first six hours. Yet at Oxford, over two-thirds of clients received major tranquillisers. This must be attributed, to a degree, to their different therapeutic philosophies, although of course it must also be linked to the higher incidence of withdrawal symptoms upon admission at Oxford. Similarly, there was clearly a policy at Tower Hamlets, where again there were more clients exhibiting withdrawal than at the designated centres, in favour of prescribing sleeping tablets (94 per cent of cases) and minor tranquillisers (92 per cent) but not major tranquillisers (8 per cent of cases). Sleeping tablets were almost always prescribed within the first six hours of admission even though only a single admission was recorded during the monitoring period after 2 p.m. on any day. This would suggest that sleeping tablets were being prescribed as a matter of policy rather than a reaction to most clients having disturbed sleep. Of course, it could be argued that Tower Hamlets and Oxford were merely acting upon their considerable experience in their field, and that had these drugs not been prescribed, then many of their clients might have suffered very uncomfortable first nights in the centres, with possibly more severe withdrawal symptoms. Although this did not occur at Leeds, where drugs were not prescribed, their client population may not have been directly comparable.

At Manchester during the monitoring period, a quarter of patients were prescribed major tranquillisers within six hours of admission, but only 14 per cent were prescribed minor tranquillisers and only 3 (2 per cent) sleeping tablets.

Within their first six hours of admission, many clients were also bathed and fed, as recorded in table 3.6. Treatment for injuries upon admission occurred very infrequently: in only five cases at Leeds, four at Oxford, two at Manchester, but never at Tower Hamlets.

Comment

The admissions procedures highlight the different policies adopted by the five centres with regard to the clients referred, the drug regimes, etc. It seems, as would be expected, that the differences in types of clients referred to the centres reflect the variations in referral

Table 3.6 Clients bathed or fed within first six hours of admission

	Leeds		Manchester		Tower Hamlets		Oxford		Portsmouth	
	No.	%	No.	%	No.	%	No.	%	No.	%
Bathed	25	17	126	89	84	94	14	11	22(11)	14
Fed	94	64	70	49	80	90	50	40	110(44)	70

procedures. The peak times for referrals by the police (to the two experimental centres) were between 9 p.m. and 8 a.m., while referrals from other sources at Manchester and the three other centres were during the daytime hours.

Again, police referrals at Leeds and Manchester were most likely to be drunk upon admission. Despite the referral system at Oxford, half the clients were drunk upon admission while the effect of the delayed admissions procedure at Tower Hamlets was that almost half the clients admitted were sober upon admission. At Portsmouth, most patients were considered by their admitting nurses to be sober on admission. Of course, it must be remembered that at Portsmouth most clients were not necessarily expected to have a drink problem. Virtually no clients at any of the centres presented acute physical problems upon admission. Very few clients required treatment for injuries upon admission, none at Manchester or Tower Hamlets, and of these only a couple at Leeds needed to be referred elsewhere for this treatment. Incidences of infestation were low at all centres, except Manchester. However, there was some indication that the detoxification centre may have been instrumental in 'cleaning up' the homeless population. Generally speaking, clients at all the centres seemed to be in a relatively good physical state. A few cases were involved in the long-term use or abuse of drugs.

The incidence of prescription of various drugs within the initial treatment period varied greatly across the centres. This may be either due to differences in prescription policies or in the psychological states of individual clients at the different centres. In Leeds, sleeping tablets and minor tranquillisers were almost never prescribed, while in Oxford, the majority of patients received major tranquillisers. However, there was a higher incidence of withdrawal symptoms upon admission at Oxford.

RESIDENCE IN DETOXIFICATION CENTRES

After the initial hours of admission, clients fitted into the day-to-day routine of the detoxification centres.

In Leeds, once the clients had sobered up, they left the holding room and moved into one of the beds within the detoxification centre proper. Clients were still free to leave at any time, but the centre programme was based on the expectation that clients would remain resident for a 10-day stay.

At Manchester, clients were moved more quickly from the holding area into one of the 'Stage I' treatment cubicles where they were all expected to remain for a minimum of 24 hours during which time their physical condition and any withdrawal symptoms were monitored closely and doctors saw them daily. They could move about the

Stage I and reception area, but could not enter the Stage II area. Most clients were moved to Stage II rooms after a day or two when they were considered well enough to get up and not in need of such concentrated medical supervision. As at Leeds, it was expected that the full detoxification programme would entail a 10-day stay.

At Tower Hamlets, after an initial stage during which clients remained in bed for 24 to 36 hours, they then entered the routine of the centre. At Tower Hamlets, the full detoxification programme was intended to run for seven days.

In Oxford, the initial admission phase moved almost immediately into the routine of the detoxification centre proper. In Oxford it was expected that clients would stop from between five and seven days, depending on their condition.

Obviously, the Portsmouth conditions were different because there was no detoxification programme as such. Patients were admitted straight into the ward and there was no fixed day programme envisaged in the general admission wards. Patients could leave at any time, but the decision to discharge a patient was the responsibility of an individual consultant, after consultation with his staff. Some patients did not enter the general admission ward but went straight into the Alcohol Treatment Unit; if patients entered this ward and needed to be dried out, they were not expected to participate in the six-week programme for the first two weeks, since it was felt they needed time to adjust.

Medical cover for residents

The effects of withdrawal

In the 1960s it was expected that one of the main functions of detoxification centres would be to cope with the effects on clients of their withdrawal from alcohol. Withdrawal symptoms, often of a serious nature, were expected to develop within a day or so of clients being admitted.

During the study period, the staff were asked to note, daily, if each resident client had exhibited any of eight indications of withdrawal, namely:

1 profuse sweating
2 marked hand tremor
3 marked body tremor
4 fits and convulsions
5 visual hallucinations
6 auditory hallucinations
7 confusion and disorientation
8 intense fear

Clients in the two designated centres had a much lower overall exhibition of withdrawal symptoms than clients in the other three

Table 3.7 Number of admissions in each centre experiencing each withdrawal symptom at least once during residence

	Leeds		Manchester		Tower Hamlets		Oxford		Portsmouth*	
	No.	%	No.	%	No.	%	No.	%	No.	%
Profuse sweating	9	6	23	15	62	64	110	89	11	26
Marked hand tremor	7	5	22	14	53	55	105	85	10	24
Marked body tremor	1	1	4	3	8	8	54	44	24	57
Fits and convulsions	1	1	1	1	0	0	5	4	10	24
Visual hallucinations	1	1	6	4	8	8	13	10	3	7
Auditory hallucinations	1	1	4	3	5	5	13	10	7	17
Confusion and disorientation	15	10	5	3	22	23	14	11	5	12
Intense fear	2	1	4	3	19	20	18	15	8	19

*Only patients admitted to *general* wards were screened out as having possible drink problems. Forms were completed for 42 out of 48 patients centres (see table 3.7); in fact this was true for each symptom. Leeds had the lowest level of reporting and Manchester the second lowest (except on 'confusion and disorientation' where the bottom two positions are reversed).

Amongst those clients at the two designated centres who did exhibit some withdrawal symptoms, they also exhibited them on fewer individual days than at the other three centres. In fact at Manchester only one client exhibited any individual symptoms on more than three individual days during their stay. More non-police referrals experienced more withdrawal symptoms than police referrals. It is not possible to make clear comparisons here with Tower Hamlets, whose normal length of stay was in any case shorter than that at Manchester, but there was a clear pattern there of most symptoms only being recorded on one occasion during the clients' stay. Thus the Tower Hamlets pattern was something like that amongst police referrals in the designated centres, although more clients exhibited more symptoms. However, the total number of symptoms at Oxford and Portsmouth and the frequency of their being repeated day by day were both much higher than at the other centres. This was perhaps a logical finding since the designated centres received drunkenness offenders; their problem upon referral by the police was that they had been drunk in public. Most clients in each centre experienced their withdrawal symptoms during the first and second days of their stay. There were two exceptions to this. Profuse sweating and hand tremor sometimes continued throughout the clients' period of residence in all centres, whilst at Portsmouth all the symptoms were sometimes exhibited beyond the second day.

Use of drugs
Prescriptions of sleeping tablets, pain killers, major and minor tranquillisers and other drugs were recorded daily. In Leeds there were few instances of drug prescriptions. During the monitoring period only five clients were ever prescribed any tranquillisers. Of the 27 clients that exhibited indications of withdrawal, only four received tranquillisers. This very sparing use of drugs was in accordance with the philosophy of the Leeds Detoxification Centre, stressed in its Operational Policy; Leeds is not included, therefore, in table 3.8.

Although not as restricted as at Leeds, the use of drugs at Manchester was restrained; however a third of admissions did receive major tranquillisers (e.g. Heminevrin). Prescriptions of major tranquillisers were made more frequently to non-police referrals (30, 45 per cent) than to police referrals (18, 21 per cent). Again the picture is one of the police referrals to designated centres being at one extreme, and the other specialist but non-designated centres not receiving drunkenness offenders at the other. At Tower Hamlets there

Table 3.8   Number of admissions where drugs were prescribed during residence

	Manchester		Tower Hamlets		Oxford		Portsmouth	
	No.	%	No.	%	No.	%	No.	%
Minor tranquillisers	21	13	95	98	8	6	8	19
Major tranquillisers	48	31	11	11	102	82	23	55
Sleeping tablets	10	6	95	98	0	–	9	21
Pain killers	6	4	13	13	2	2	6	14
Others	48	31	95	98	56	45	25	60
Any drug	124	79	97	100	115	93	38	90
No drugs	29	18	0	–	9	7	4	10

was blanket usage of minor tranquillisers and sleeping tablets, whilst Oxford prescribed 102 (82 per cent) patients with major tranquillisers. Over half the clients in Oxford were prescribed major tranquillisers on three or more days of their residence. This, of course, should be related to the much higher incidence of withdrawal symptoms at Oxford. In Portsmouth over half the people admitted as having a probable alcohol problem also received major tranquillisers with over five prescriptions each on average during their stay.

Medical cover by doctors
At Leeds it was initially envisaged that there would be daily GP attendance under the general direction of the consultant psychiatrist who would set the overall treatment regime. It was expected that GPs would check patients on or soon after admission. However, it was found in practice that GP cover was below that envisaged in the operational policy. During the monitoring period, one doctor attended the centre twice a week and another once. These doctors attempted to make a routine examination of any men admitted for the first time a day or so after their admission and to see other men as and when men requested it or following a nurse's recommendation. However, the daily check form study in Leeds showed that of 86

residents making 146 residences or part-residences during the monitoring period, only 17 routine examinations (20 per cent) were recorded as having occurred and 32 check-ups (37 per cent) for specific complaints. In part this may have been because the operational policy's ideas were not realistic in practice since some men were admitted very many times with little time between each admission. It would be understandable if it was not felt necessary to routinely examine such persons upon every visit. However, GPs were also unable to see all new admissions because many of them left early. During the study period, 31 clients made their first admission, but only 9 (29 per cent) of them were examined by a doctor. All but two of the others left within 24 hours; those two stayed for three days but were not available when the doctor arrived at the centre. During the monitoring period, 17 appointments with the doctor did not take place because the men were out while the GPs were at the centre.

The Tower Hamlets Detoxification Centre attempted to run a similar sort of medical cover programme, but because men there stayed longer and were unable to go out of the centre prior to discharge, the medical cover programme could be applied much more methodically. There were two visiting doctors, one of whom came on Sunday mornings, and another on Wednesday afternoons. Therefore any client who had stayed at least three days was given a full medical check-up on one of these occasions. As far as can be seen from the data collection, each client who was available to be checked did indeed see the doctor, and thus 81 out of 97 men (84 per cent) admitted during the monitoring period received a routine check-up. Three of these men also saw one of the doctors for a specific problem in addition to their routine check-up. There was more comprehensive medical cover in the hospital-based centres. The Manchester Detoxification Centre made a full examination and investigation of all admissions soon after their arrival at the centre. Besides this initial admission check-up, 29 persons were also checked after this point, and another 24 also received treatment for some specific problem at some point during their stay.

There was even greater cover at Oxford, where patients were seen within the first couple of hours for a full examination, and then routinely reviewed by a doctor each morning. The doctors also used these check-ups to begin eliciting discussion and treatment of any other problems the patients might have had, and patients were encouraged to discuss their problems with the doctor at the morning meeting. Thus within the 12-week monitoring period at Oxford, 465 instances were recorded of medical check-ups on patients, even though there were only 124 admissions within this period. Thus each admission at Oxford saw a doctor on average nearly four times during his/her stay. Psychiatric expertise was also available at Manchester where 237 consultations were recorded. This compared with a mere seven at Leeds and no psychiatric cover whatsoever at Tower Hamlets.

Thus in Manchester patients were given a routine check-up soon after admission, over half the admissions were seen by a psychiatrist on their first day, and three-quarters were seen within the first two days of their residence. At Oxford, doctor/patient interactions were very high over the whole of the expected five-day programme. However, at Tower Hamlets, there was no pattern because there was no daily cover. At Leeds the pattern of medical cover was even more haphazard as a result of the rapid turnover of clients and the relatively small amount of cover by doctors.

Ancillary medical services
Referrals to ancillary medical services such as dentist, optician and chiropodist were rare. A few clients at Leeds and Manchester were referred to these services. However, no referrals were made in Tower Hamlets, surprisingly for a relatively unsettled population. Referrals outside the detoxification centres for other types of treatment and help were relatively infrequent. The only centre to do so on a somewhat regular basis was Manchester. When clients were referred to another part of Withington Hospital for medical treatment, it was usually to have an X-ray conducted, and this in turn was usually of the chest. Referrals to other medical facilities tended to be for alcohol-related problems, notably pancreatitis. Other types of help involving referrals out of the detoxification centre were to the Manchester Royal Eye Hospital for treatment on detached retinas, referrals to the Alcohol Treatment Unit and to various hostels for initial assessments.

Comment

Clients at Leeds and Manchester reported the lowest incidence of individual withdrawal symptoms. Clients at the two designated centres who did exhibit some withdrawal symptoms also exhibited them on fewer individual days than at the other three centres. In Manchester, non-police referrals experienced more withdrawal symptoms than police referrals. Perhaps this was because the designated centres received drunkenness offenders; their problem upon referral by the police was that they had been drunk in public. This did not guarantee that they either had an ongoing drink problem or that they were going to have any noticeable withdrawal symptoms while sobering up. At the other centres, however, referrals were planned and the person's need for detoxification had been assessed and accepted.

Moreover it would be expected that such referrals would be in a more serious withdrawal state when sent to a hospital than to a community-based centre. Since Oxford accepted only patients specifically referred for detoxification, it was to be expected that it would encounter the greatest incidence of withdrawal symptoms. In a way, Oxford was the 'purest' example of a detoxification centre in the sense of drying people out under supervision and not attempting to achieve other immediate goals besides this.

The use of drugs in Leeds was minimal. Although not as restricted at Leeds, the use of drugs at Manchester was restrained. At Tower Hamlets, there was blanket usage of minor tranquillisers and sleeping tablets, while Oxford administered most patients with major tranquillisers. Over half the patients admitted to general admission wards in Portsmouth with a probable alcohol problem also received major tranquillisers.

There was a very considerable difference in medical cover between the hospital-based detoxification centres and the community-based detoxification centres which relied on visiting doctors. Naturally medical cover by doctors was greatest in the hospital-based detoxification centres. Yet the type of client likely to be admitted to Leeds and Tower Hamlets — namely, men of no fixed abode — are known to have greater primary health care problems on average than most people, and to have a high incidence of psychiatric problems. Unfortunately, only the hospital-based centres could rapidly and systematically offer routine check-ups, psychiatric care and primary health care and relate this to the general treatment programme.

PRACTICAL HELP AND EMOTIONAL SUPPORT

Although all the centres agreed on the necessity of offering help and emotional support, they varied as to how much, when, how and by whom. Factors which appeared to determine differences between centres were resources, type of staff, treatment approach of any parent agency, alternative facilities provided elsewhere and assumptions about the nature of their clients' problems. For example, the nature and number of staff responsible for providing practical help and emotional support varied considerably. Each centre except Oxford had social workers. The number, and amount of their time available, differed from centre to centre.

All the centres except Oxford ran either daily or weekly groups. The nature and purpose of these ranged from a weekly information-giving group at Tower Hamlets, to daily group therapy (including weekends) at Manchester. The Tower Hamlets group was run by the full-time social worker, while the group at Manchester was run by nurses and those in Portsmouth and Leeds by different staff groups.

At Tower Hamlets, Manchester and Nelson Ward (Portsmouth) groups were compulsory while those at Portsmouth (general wards) and Leeds were not.

Leeds

Sixty-one men (70 per cent) had had formal/informal contact with their social worker during their stay. Fifty-six per cent of the total contact time was concerned with practical matters and 44 per cent with casework issues (e.g. anxiety, motivation, interpersonal difficulties and drinking). Where possible men, when discharged, were followed up.

Manchester

Forty-eight per cent of admissions (74) had at least one discussion session with the social worker at the centre. The most common reasons for discussion sessions were: after-care arrangements, accommodation, and casework on drinking and personal problems; and social workers often made arrangements for accommodation or after-care on discharge and entitlements to benefits. The social workers also had informal contact with clients, as did all the other staff groups.

The brief of the two social workers extended beyond the detoxification centre. They were responsible for supporting ex-patients. They also had a development role and regularly visited the various local agencies for single homeless and problem drinkers.

Tower Hamlets

Ninety-eight per cent of admissions (95) had at least one discussion session with the full-time social worker or officer in charge. The majority of discussion sessions and arrangements happened in the days close to admission. These focused primarily on practical matters such as accommodation, employment and money, as well as on casework on drinking and personal problems. The arrangements made were mostly concerned with admission into the detoxification centre and accommodation or after-care after discharge. The care assistants had a lot of informal contact with the men.

Oxford

All staff counselled the detoxification patients; they also did assessment interviews at which they did the majority of formal counselling and made appropriate discharge arrangements. After this, contact with staff was likely to be much more informal. The amount of time given over to counselling depended very much on patient demand.

The subjects under discussion ranged from the details of discharge arrangements to acute personal problems such as bereavement. Patients were expected to take responsibility for themselves at discharge and only rely on staff to make arrangements when this was the most practical thing to do. Hence, less time was spent on giving practical assistance than on emotional support.

Portsmouth

There was a social worker attached to each ward team, except Nelson Ward. (Some social workers were full-time, others were not.) Case allocation was determined by individual social workers in consultation with their ward teams and consultants. If a patient was already attached to a local authority social worker, the patient was not allocated; however it was expected that the social worker would be informed of the patient's presence at the hospital.

During the 12-week monitoring period, eight patients (22 per cent) with drinking problems were seen by two social workers; all but one patient was seen by a single social worker. Also during this time one problem drinker was referred to his/her local authority social worker.

The few that were seen were assisted on a range of practical matters and nearly always had arrangements made for them. Help, too, was given with personal problems although not with problems with drinking.

All patients in the general wards were expected to attend occupational therapy daily, when fit.

The information collected from ward staff suggested that problem drinkers had at least as much opportunity as non-problem drinkers to discuss issues with ward staff and have arrangements made for them. However, how much time was spent on drinking problems per se clearly varied across wards, as did the emphasis on discussion as opposed to arrangements, and attendance at ward meetings.

Comment

The centres in Leeds and Manchester were similar: both had structured and intensive programmes (including daily groups, one-to-one counselling, etc.) which aimed at, or at least aimed at initiating, a change in clients' drinking behaviour. Oxford and Tower Hamlets and the general wards at Portsmouth offered referral to treatment, but not treatment itself.

Although the centres varied as to how they responded to the emotional and practical needs of problem drinkers, they can at least be grouped in terms of the nature of their operation. They all attempted to assess the clients' problems and in various ways, to give support, shelter and immediate help with practical problems, but they differed as to what further they could expect to achieve. In the non-designated centres clients were referred on to treatment or rehabilitation facilities. In the designated centres these processes began prior to making such referrals.

Another operational feature in Manchester and Leeds was the use of staff to follow up clients who had left, and in order to try and maintain relationships that had been built up with them, by the staff; while in Oxford, Tower Hamlets and Portsmouth, appointment systems, day programmes or out-patient clinics were used instead. The advantage of follow-up workers over these arrangements was that they would be able to keep in touch with those unable or not motivated to keep appointments.

It is not possible at this stage to gauge how effective any of the help might have been; however, the findings, for example, at Leeds were that few residents attended many of the group sessions during their stay. This suggests that whatever is offered at that centre may well not be utilised.

PATIENT ACTIVITIES

In a pilot study in Leeds clients felt they were left with too much spare time and reported feeling bored, although they valued the warmth and companionship of the other residents. In Manchester, Tower Hamlets and Oxford, patients all had some responsibility for domestic tasks, particularly making beds, cleaning rooms and washing. (It was not feasible to monitor patient activities in Portsmouth since there was no specific centre for clientele and each ward ran slightly different regimes.) As in Leeds, clients at the three other centres were left with much spare time since their 'chores' or 'duties' in most cases took up less than an hour of their time. Most of this time was spent talking to other clients or to members of staff. Interaction with staff appears, as would be expected, to be dependent on the number of staff available; thus patient/staff contact was lowest in Tower Hamlets and highest in Manchester. Another difference between the four centres was that in accordance with the rules applied in Manchester, Oxford and Tower Hamlets, clients could not leave the centre during their stay unless it was necessary for their treatment (such as to go to other hospitals, etc.) while in Leeds, clients were free to go out during the day so long as they did not drink.

DISCHARGE AND REFERRAL OUT

(This was not monitored at Manchester as this would have replicated a study of discharge and follow-up that had been done by a member of the centre staff (Makanjuola, 1981.)

Much stress was placed by the centre staff and others on what happened to clients after sobering up. Merely to sober up habitual drunkenness offenders could not be expected to divert them from the penal system in any meaningful way. Similarly, the non-designated centres stressed in their goal statements that sobering up was but the first stage of their work. The profiles of the centres indicate the emphasis staff put on assessment and referral, in effect on detoxification facilities as access points for the problem drinker (be they habitual drunkenness offenders or not), to services which have the function of providing housing, treatment and support.

Leeds

Clients were most frequently referred to rooms, bedsits, etc.; and somewhat less frequently to rehabilitation or treatment facilities or common lodging-houses or hostels. The clients did not always reach their planned discharge destination. In fact only 28 per cent of clients left as planned. The five after-care beds were used to hold residents while referral arrangements were being made.

Tower Hamlets

Of those who were NFA (no fixed abode) on admission, just under half were discharged to Salvation Army common lodging-houses or hostels. Those who came from fixed abodes returned there, apart from those referred to residential projects. Those who had been NFA were more likely to be sent to rehabilitation hostels (11 per cent) and Salvation Army centres (15 per cent) than those of fixed abode. They were also more likely to have arrangements made for non-residential treatment.

Oxford

Most of the clients (69 per cent) left to go to a bedsit or flat on discharge. Arrangements for residential treatment or rehabilitation were only made for six people, four of whom were referred to an ATU. However, the majority (71 per cent) did have some kind of appointment made for them, which was either a follow-up visit by ward staff or an out-patient appointment with a view to assessment for admission to the Ley Clinic or attendance at the day programme.

No residential treatment or rehabilitation was arranged for any of the 19 NFA clients. The tendency was for these patients to be offered out-patient appointments with a view to attendance at the day programme or follow-up visits by ward staff. The majority of those of fixed abode were offered follow-up visits by ward staff and contact with community nursing staff.

Portsmouth

Of the 27 patients in the general wards identified by the screening as being likely to have a drink problem, five were referred for residential treatment, usually to Nelson Ward. Non-residential treatment or rehabilitation arrangements were made for 13 (48 per cent) of the problem drinkers compared to 62 per cent of the non-problem drinkers.

At Nelson Ward, where drying out was occasionally done, none of the patients discharged went to any form of residential facility and a few were referred for non-residential help.

Comment

The four centres (Leeds, Oxford, Tower Hamlets and Portsmouth) reflected a variety of patterns of referral out and therefore of access to specialist and non-specialist services. The nature of the variation seems to derive from the particular system or organisation of which a centre was a part. This system bias was reflected, for example, at Tower Hamlets, by staff's tendency to refer to Salvation Army facilities, at Leeds to their own residential hostels, at Portsmouth and Oxford to their respective out-patients departments and ATUs. The tendency was therefore to match people to immediately available services rather than services to individuals' needs. The extent of bias towards 'own' organisations differed. Tower Hamlets was situated close to a number of specialist projects for problem drinkers run by other non-statutory organisations and was in close touch with them; however little use was made of them. Leeds relied heavily on their project houses yet did refer to some other projects.

It is noticeable that even when residential facilities were available, very few people were referred to them. The limited use made of them by Leeds and Tower Hamlets indicated that this form of provision was either inappropriate as a direct step after detoxification for most people or that these facilities were in fact designed to cater for a specific small group only; that is those who are articulate and able to function in a communal setting. Problems too may have arisen because bed vacancies were unlikely to occur as quickly as a centre's turnover required them.

There is some indication that clients of specialist centres benefited from this specialism. Their clients were offered a wider range of discharge opportunities than were patients in Portsmouth where fewer specialist community facilities had been developed.

It was apparent that staff at many of the centres did not know whether a majority of those with arrangements made for them on discharge made use of them or not. (This was not the case at Manchester where information was collected for a research study.) If this lack of contact continued beyond the point of discharge, questions could be raised about continuity of care of problem drinkers across agencies and of centres' commitment to this in practice. It may have been that the centres saw continuity of care as important but did not have sufficient resources to do what would have to be done.

CONCLUSIONS

The extent and severity of withdrawal symptoms amongst clients admitted to the designated centres were much less than had initially been envisaged by the Weiler Report. As such the requirements for medical treatment and high levels of medical staff were not as great as in Oxford where the clients had more severe withdrawal symptoms.

Nevertheless clients admitted to the designated centres were in need of assistance in dealing with more social problems, such as financial, accommodation, employment and personal problems. This was the case for all the homeless and quasi-homeless clients at any of the centres; however not all the centres had the staff to deal with such matters.

The referral system into a detoxification centre to a great extent defined the requirements for type and level of staffing, care provisions and accessibility for clients. It is quite clear that where police referrals were in operation, 24-hour access was almost essential; clients were more likely to be drunk but not experiencing severe withdrawals, and a much greater number of admissions could be expected. In non-designated centres similar in nature to that in Oxford, admission times can be restricted as admissions will most likely be planned. Clients are likely to require more medical supervision for withdrawals but less assistance with practical/social problems.

None of the centres placed much emphasis on patient activities. In fact in most cases they were treated more like physically ill patients and not allowed to leave the building. Once they had recovered from any withdrawal symptoms that they might have had clients tended to find that there was little to do.

It can perhaps be concluded that there is more than one type of client requiring detoxification – those with acute problems and those with chronic problems. The extent of the problem is obviously greater than that outlined in the Weiler Report. The apparent differences in requirements of the different potential client groups indicates that more than one type of service should be provided.

4
Characteristics of Clients

As explained in the Introduction, detoxification centres in Britain have most often been conceived as responses to habitual drunkenness offending, which in turn has been presumed to occur largely amongst single homeless males. Yet our initial visits, even to the experimental centres accepting only police referrals of people apprehended for drunkenness, did not indicate that all clients were exclusively homeless or had all committed drunkenness offences in the past. The other centres which did not accept police referrals seemed even more likely to deal with other types of client. Besides homeless drunkenness offenders, they dealt with females, with home-based drinkers, and with people who had *never* committed any drunkenness offences.

It was clearly important then to get some clearer profile of the clientele of detoxification centres. Unfortunately, it proved impossible to get sufficient or reliable data from official records such as criminal records, Department of Employment records, the National Psychiatric Register and so on. It was particularly difficult to trace records of homeless clients, or to be confident about the validity of those relatively few records which could be found.

Therefore data had to be collected on individual client characteristics by interviewing samples of residents within detoxification centres. The research assistant in each centre (except Portsmouth) interviewed every new client admitted within a 15-week period, using a standardised schedule which took 45 to 60 minutes to complete. Clients could not be interviewed until the staff considered they were fit enough to do so, and in most cases this was not until about three days subsequent to admission. This was unfortunate at Leeds, since some clients left before this time (although some of these were interviewed during subsequent longer stays). Leeds residents could also leave the premises during the day. Together with the higher repeating rates at Leeds, these factors made the number of individual clients interviewed at Leeds less than might have been expected.

At Portsmouth, it was obviously inappropriate to interview all patients admitted over a 15-week period, since only a minority of them would have had drinking problems. Thus all the patients whom

Table 4.1 Numbers interviewed at each centre

	Leeds		Manchester		Tower Hamlets		Oxford		Portsmouth	
	No.	%	No.	%	No.	%	No.	%	No.	%
Male	68	100.0	90 (34)	85.7	82	100.0	56	71.8	33	68.8
Female	0	0	15 (8)	14.3	0	0	22	28.2	15	31.3

Figures in brackets denote police referrals. There was no significant difference in the sex ratio of police referrals compared to all referrals

Table 4.2 Age distribution of clients

	Leeds		Manchester		Tower Hamlets		Oxford		Portsmouth	
	No.	%	No.	%	No.	%	No.	%	No.	%
25 years or less	6	8.8	8	7.6	3	3.7	4	5.1	4	8.3
26–35 years	9	13.2	30	28.6	20	24.4	24	30.8	13	27.1
36–45 years	25	36.8	37	35.2	35	42.7	14	17.9	20	41.7
46–55 years	12	17.6	15	14.3	16	19.5	24	30.8	9	18.8
56–65 years	15	22.1	12	11.4	7	8.5	10	12.8	2	4.2
65 + years	1	1.5	3	2.9	1	1.2	2	2.6	0	0

the screening methods indicated were problem drinkers were interviewed during a six-month period (see table 4.1). Table 4.2 shows
Leeds and Tower Hamlets had older clientele than the hospital
centres. It suggests that detoxification centres receiving police referrals and homeless males tended to have older client populations, and
indeed at Manchester 41 per cent of police referrals were over 45,
compared to only 21 per cent of referrals from other sources.

Each client completed a series of questions used before in alcoholic
hostels to assess degrees of previous social stability (Otto and
Orford, 1979). Clients were graded by this scale into high, medium
and low previous social stability. The non-designated hospital
centres recorded high levels of client stability, and police referrals the
lowest (see table 4.3).

At Leeds no client was married and living with his wife. There was
only one at Tower Hamlets, and one among police referrals to
Manchester. Yet at Oxford and Portsmouth, 35 per cent and 40 per
cent respectively were married and living with their spouse. Indeed
despite the higher age of populations at Leeds, Manchester and
Tower Hamlets, 38 per cent in each of these centres had never been
married, compared to only 19 per cent at Oxford and a mere 15 per
cent at Portsmouth. Yet despite this, Leeds, Manchester and Tower
Hamlets also had higher proportions of clients who were separated
or divorced.

Seventy-eight per cent of Leeds clients had no contact with any
relatives in the month prior to interview and over a third reported
they had not had any contact with any relatives for over five years.

The Leeds population were considerably more socially isolated
than any of the other groups; Tower Hamlets and Manchester police
referrals being of a similar but less extreme nature.

Besides the overall demographic characteristics of clients, data
were collected to assess the clients' functioning within the three-
months period after admission to the detoxification centres, and in
more detail about the seven days before admission.

FUNCTIONING IN THE THREE MONTHS PRIOR TO ADMISSION

In the three months before admission, clients at Leeds were the least
likely to have received any wages (13 per cent) with successively
larger proportions having had wages at Manchester, Tower Hamlets, Oxford and the highest at Portsmouth (42 per cent). The positions of the centres were exactly reversed in terms of proportions of
clients having received supplementary benefit from 25 per cent at
Portsmouth up to 47 per cent at Leeds. Although clients at Tower
Hamlets were more likely than police referrals to Leeds and Man-

Table 4.3 Social stability scores for clients at each centre

Degree of stability	Leeds		Manchester		Tower Hamlets		Oxford		Portsmouth	
	No.	%	No.	%	No.	%	No.	%	No.	%
Low	16	23.5	20 (10)	19.0 (23.8)	12	14.6	7	9.0	4	8.3
Medium	25	36.8	27 (9)	25.7 (21.4)	30	36.6	13	16.7	14	29.2
High	27	39.7	58 (23)	55.2 (54.8)	40	48.8	58	74.4	30	62.5

Figures in brackets denote police referrals

chester to have received wages, it was clear that most of these wages had been received for casual labour. Nearly half of them had worked casually within the three months prior to interview, 23 per cent for ten days or more, compared with only small percentages of clients at other centres.

Similar proportions had been sleeping rough prior to admission to Leeds (56 per cent, 31 per cent for more than ten days) and Tower Hamlets (59 per cent, 39 per cent for more than ten days). At the other centres, which did not cater exclusively for homeless single males, the proportions were still considerable: 15 per cent at Portsmouth, 25 per cent at Oxford and 38 per cent at Manchester.

A similar pattern applied to clients having changed accommodation. Two-thirds of police referrals to Leeds and Manchester and the clients at Tower Hamlets had changed accommodation at least once during the three months prior to admission; over a quarter, three to six times; and between 11 per cent and 14 per cent at each centre more than six times. However, only nine clients in total at Oxford and Portsmouth had changed accommodation more than three times. Portsmouth and Oxford clients were also much less likely to have spent any time outside their respective areas.

FUNCTIONING IN THE SEVEN DAYS PRIOR TO ADMISSION

As might be expected, clients admitted to all the centres had not been working or living in favourable circumstances in the week prior to admission. Sixty-nine per cent at Portsmouth and over 80 per cent at the other four centres had not worked in the seven days prior to admission. Three-quarters of clients admitted by the police to Leeds, Tower Hamlets and Manchester had not seen any relatives during this period, and between a quarter and two-thirds of clients at each centre had not had a cooked meal for seven days. Although on average Tower Hamlets clients were not as chronically disadvantaged as police referrals, they were in the most acute trouble upon admission. Tower Hamlets had the highest proportion without a meal for seven days (63 per cent) and living off supplementary benefit (45 per cent), the lowest proportion with income from other sources, and the least contact with relatives. Moreover, 35 per cent of Tower Hamlets clients stated that in the seven days prior to admission they had wanted, but had been unable to receive, medical treatment, many more than at any of the other centres. It is ironic that Tower Hamlets had the least amount of medical cover of any of the five centres.

This higher problem level amongst Tower Hamlets clients is an important point, because it seemed to be providing the most acutely needed service, yet was the least well resourced, because it did not fit into either an NHS-based medical response or into the theory of responding to drunkenness offenders.

The level of immediate problems upon admission to Tower Hamlets cast doubt on the idea that detoxification centres for drunkenness offenders had the advantage of contacting persons at a particularly stressful point in their drinking career when they might be more willing to consider their problems and accept treatment. Although it seems clients brought by the police to Leeds and to Manchester were more chronically disadvantaged than clients referred to Tower Hamlets, nevertheless at the time of their admission, Tower Hamlets' clients might have been more willing to seek treatment than clients at the designated centres. Of course the Tower Hamlets centre stressed the need for motivation on the part of men hoping to be admitted there.

At Tower Hamlets and Leeds 32 per cent spent the night previous to admission either squatting or sleeping rough. This also occurred to a degree at Manchester but much less at Oxford (9 per cent) and in only one case at Portsmouth.

At Leeds and Tower Hamlets, men who had not been squatting or sleeping rough on the night previous to their admission had often spent that night in various types of hostels, reception centre, shelters and other such institutions. But two-thirds of Oxford and Portsmouth referrals had spent the night previous to admission at their home address, with only tiny numbers registered as having spent the night at institutions typically frequented by homeless persons.

This highlights the opening point made in this chapter – that ideas about who would constitute target populations of detoxification centres have been confused. Throughout the Weiler Report (1971) and other associated literature ran the implicit assumption that problem drinkers, habitual drunkenness offenders and the homeless were one and the same group. Yet logically these could be separate groups, although they obviously overlap. Part of the client characteristic interviews was therefore designed to assess how far clients within the five different detoxification centres were:

- habitual drunkenness offenders
- problem drinkers
- homeless

HOW MANY CLIENTS WERE HABITUAL DRUNKENNESS OFFENDERS?

There was no guarantee in any of the five centres that any person brought to them would necessarily be an habitual drunkenness offender. Manchester's admission criteria did not require clients to

Table 4.4 Pattern of drunkenness offending amongst sample of clients at each centre

	No. of 3 + offenders	% of each centre's clients	No. of 1–2 offenders	%	No. of non-offenders	%
Leeds	56	82.3	5	7.4	5	7.4
Manchester	60 (27)	57.1 (64.3)	16 (6)	15.2 (14.3)	28 (9)	26.7 (21.4)
Tower Hamlets	44	53.7	18	22.0	20	24.4
Oxford	20	25.6	25	32.1	33	42.3
Portsmouth	9	18.8	13	27.1	26	50.2

Figures in brackets denote police referrals

have had a previous drunkenness conviction. At Leeds the admission criteria restricted the target population to single homeless males arrested for drunkenness but they did not have to have had any previous offences. At the other centres clients might never have committed *any* drunkenness offences. The pattern of drunkenness offending amongst the sample of interviewed clients, set out in table 4.4, splits clients into those who had committed three or more offences (habitual offenders), one or two offences (occasional offenders), and those who had never been arrested drunk.

It should be remembered that the Leeds sample under-represented clients who left the centre early in the programme and as far as could be gathered from Leeds court records, early-leaving non-repeating clients were not habitual drunkenness offenders. Although Leeds had the most problems with clients leaving early, it should be remembered that this centre also had the least control over who was brought there. The other centres had considerable choice in all or at least some of their admissions. Many of those who left Leeds early were not part of the target population and did not require what the centre had been set up to provide. This would be inevitable in any emergency system in which no referrals ever came from medical or social work agencies. Yet the clients who *did* remain for most of the programme at Leeds comprised the highest proportion of offenders of any of the five centres.

A quarter of Tower Hamlets and Manchester clients, nearly half Oxford clients and over half Portsmouth clients had *never* committed a drunkenness offence. Yet at Leeds 60 per cent of clients who completed the interview had committed over 10 drunken offences (see table 4.5).

Table 4.5   Pattern of drunkenness offending by sex (all centres combined)

	3 + habitual drunkenness offences		1—2 drunkenness offences		0 offences	
	N = 190		N = 77		N = 112	
	No.	%	No.	%	No.	%
Male	181	95.3	68	88.3	78	69.6
Female	9	4.7	9	11.7	34	30.4

The only female habitual drunkenness offenders were two at Oxford and Portsmouth and five at Manchester (all five were brought by the police). Manchester was the only designated centre to which police could take female drunkenness offenders and only eight were referred in total during the 15-week interviewing period.

No relationship between drunkenness offending and age was found at any of the centres or in the combined data.

It should not be automatically assumed that habitual drunkenness offenders were necessarily homeless. At Leeds, seven habitual drunkenness offenders (12 per cent) and at Manchester six (22 per cent) brought by the police and 12 clients (36 per cent) from other referral sources had spent the night previous to their arrest at a home address.

HOW MANY CLIENTS WERE PROBLEM DRINKERS?

It cannot be assumed that a client of a detoxification centre inevitably had a drink problem. As far as it was possible to judge, many clients admitted only once to Leeds who left quickly were probably not problem drinkers. Some may have been brought by the police because they appeared drunk when their actual problem was a drug overdose, mental illness, brain damage or some other condition. Some may have been brought for some problem, such as threatening suicide or having an injury, which the police felt might be better dealt with by the detoxification centre staff than at other ostensibly more appropriate agencies. Apart from early leavers, all other clients at all centres appeared to have an ongoing drink problem.

According to the classic studies of Jellinek (1952, 1960), the crucial watershed on the way to becoming an 'alcoholic' was a 'block amnesia', i.e. waking up after a drinking session in a strange locale with no idea of what had happened the night before or how they had got there. All but two clients at Leeds and Tower Hamlets reported this experience as did 87 per cent at Manchester, 80 per cent at Oxford and 63 per cent at Portsmouth. This concurred with the results of the Severity of Alcohol Dependence Questionnaire (Hodgson, R. et al., 1978) completed by each interviewed client. This attempted to rate the degree of 'dependence on alcohol' by asking if during a recent heavy drinking period the client had experienced any of 20 items, such as shaky hands, fears upon waking after drinking, and so on. These were divided into five sections of four items each. The sections were created to indicate:

- physical withdrawal symptoms
- psychological withdrawal symptoms
- relief drinking (i.e. drinking to avert withdrawal symptoms)

- excessive consumption
- rapid reinstatement of withdrawal symptoms after periods of abstinence

The clients were asked if they had experienced each item never, occasionally, sometimes, or regularly.

Although there were deviations within the populations, and some internal inconsistency between individual scores on the various sections, overall mean scores concurred with the other data in providing a rough guide to the degree of overall problem drinking in each client population. The mean scores were highest at Tower Hamlets (42.5) followed by Manchester (39.9 police referrals, 36.4 others), Leeds (36.1), Oxford (30.8) and Portsmouth (24.9). These were all higher scores than were recorded amongst Portsmouth patients admitted to the Alcohol Treatment Unit with an unequivocal drink problem, who only scored 24.1 on average. Clearly, then, the populations as a whole had a high level of problem drinking, and everyone but one or two clients could discuss the questionnaire in terms of a recent period of heavy drinking.

The differences between the centres could not be explained in terms of different elements of the questionnaire. The questions on consumption, followed by relief drinking, scored highest in each population.

HOW MANY CLIENTS WERE HOMELESS?

Homelessness is not a precise condition, but rather a continuum. Clients were classified into two types by the following criteria:

Chronic homeless (or Skid Row)

1 Those with a low score of previous social stability, which indicated having left home and using cheap accommodation or reception centres at an early age, frequently changing accommodation and employment, and having had an early conviction for an offence (other than drunkenness), and/or

2 Clients who:

(a) had no contact with relatives over the last five years *and*,

(b) had slept rough for 10 days or more in the past few months, *and*,

(c) had ever drunk surgical or methylated spirits.

Acute homeless

Any client who had spent any of the three nights prior to admission squatting or sleeping rough, or in a reception centre, Salvation Army hostel, Church Army hostel or any similar institution.

Table 4.6 Pattern of homelessness amongst clients at each centre

No. of homeless clients	Leeds		Manchester		Tower Hamlets		Oxford		Portsmouth		TOTAL
	No.	%	No.	%	No.	%	No.	%	No.	%	
Chronic	20	29	21 (10)	20	13	16	7	9	4	8	65
Acute	38	56	30 (21)	48 (50)	60	73	18	23	5	10	172
Total	41	60	58	55	62	76	20	26	8	17	192

Figures in brackets denote police referrals

Total homeless

Most, but not all the chronic homeless were also contained within the acute homeless group, so table 4.6 also gives a total homeless category of all acute and/or chronic homeless clients. Virtually none of these were female, but, surprisingly perhaps, there was no relationship between homelessness and age.

Most of the homeless were either unmarried (Tower Hamlets, Manchester and Leeds), or separated or divorced (Oxford and Portsmouth). The chronic homeless had much heavier use of both prescribed and non-prescribed drugs than other clients. They also had more convictions for drunkenness, mostly committed outside the area.

In the three months before their admission, their life-style had been characterised by drinking surgical spirits and meths, using cheap accommodation and sleeping rough.

The distinctions between types of homelessness show that Leeds, Manchester, and Tower Hamlets admitted many more homeless clients than the other two centres but that again acute homelessness was most prevalent at Tower Hamlets, whilst the chronic condition was worst at Leeds and then Manchester.

WHAT WAS THE RELATIONSHIP BETWEEN PROBLEM DRINKING, HABITUAL DRUNKENNESS OFFENDING AND HOMELESSNESS?

In each centre there were different degrees of problem drinking, drunkenness offending and homelessness. How far did these overlap?

The highest incidence of withdrawal symptoms and the heaviest use of drugs was recorded at Oxford. Since Oxford clientele were not measured as having a generally more severe or developed drinking problem, the level of acute problem must have been higher there. Oxford clients also had shorter treatment histories. Their problems were probably at an earlier stage, and they had less experience of coping with withdrawal. It may also have been that their drinking pattern was different. Populations such as that at Oxford where three-quarters were home based, with more financial resources, and including more women, might have been 'binge' type drinkers who had recently engaged in particularly heavy consumption.

The next highest incidence of withdrawal was at Tower Hamlets which admitted largely homeless and rootless men. But it has been pointed out that this centre was more likely than the others to admit clients going through an acute crisis of functioning. It would appear therefore that the different distribution of withdrawal across the centres was explicable in terms of the different reasons how and why clients became admitted to them at particular times.

Secondly, there were differences in degree of severity of drinking problem between clients. When the Severity of Alcohol Dependence Questionnaire (SADQ) (Hodgson, 1978) scores were pooled across the centres, clients who were habitual drunkenness offenders scored highest, clients who had been arrested drunk once or twice scored medium, and non-offenders scored least. Furthermore, as table 4.7 demonstrates, this pattern applied to each of the five subsections of the questionnaire.

Table 4.7   Relationship between problem drinking and patterns of drunkenness offending

	Habitual 3 + offenders	Occasional (1 or 2) offenders	Non (0) offenders
	N = 190	N = 77	N = 112
Physical withdrawal	7.8	6.2	5.0
Psychological withdrawal	6.6	4.9	4.6
Relief drinking	9.3	7.5	6.5
Alcohol consumption	8.9	7.9	7.0
Reinstatement after abstinence	7.7	6.1	5.5
Total dependence score	40.3	32.6	28.6

The correlation between number of drunkenness offences and severity of drinking problem was further confirmed by three questions asked in addition to the SADQ (see table 4.8).

The more drunkenness offences clients reported, the more they also reported previous treatment for drinking problems (see table 4.9).

This all confirms the studies of drunkenness offenders assembled in the Weiler Report which indicated that habitual offenders were problem drinkers. The possibility that anyone could be an *habitual* drunkenness offender without having serious problems with drink must be remote.

There was also an inverse relationship between social stability and drunkenness offending. It was particularly rare for anyone in the

Table 4.8 Relationship between severity of drinking problem and patterns of drunkenness offending

	Habitual (3+) offenders		Occasional (1 or 2) offenders		Non (0) offenders	
	N = 190		N = 77		N = 112	
	No.	%	No.	%	No.	%
Have you ever:						
woken up after drinking with no idea how you got there?	186	97.9	67	87.0	74	66.1
imagined seeing or hearing things due to drink?	157	82.6	43	56.8	50	44.6
drunk surgical or methylated spirits?	101	53.2	13	16.9	9	8.0

Table 4.9 Relationship between previous treatment and pattern of drunkenness offending

	Habitual (3+) offenders		Occasional (1 or 2) offenders		Non (0) offenders	
	N = 190		N = 77		N = 112	
	No.	%	No.	%	No.	%
Rehabilitation hostel	54	28.4	7	9.1	9	8.0
In-patient alcoholism treatment	114	60.0	39	50.6	51	45.5
Out-patient alcoholism treatment	47	24.7	22	28.6	24	21.4
AA meetings	157	82.6	39	50.6	48	42.9

Table 4.10 Relationship between social stability score and patterns of drunkenness offending

Previous social stability score	Habitual (3 +) offenders		Occasional (1 or 2) offenders		Non (0) offenders	
	N = 190		N = 77		N = 112	
	No.	%	No.	%	No.	%
Low	47	24.7	10	13.0	2	1.8
Medium	73	38.4	13	16.9	22	19.6
High	70	36.8	54	70.1	88	78.6

samples to report low previous social stability without having become a drunkenness offender (see table 4.10).

But although there was a general relationship between homelessness and drunkenness offending, it did not apply in each individual case, particularly as regarded habitual offending. Across all five centres, one-third of habitual drunkenness offenders were home-based, and one-third of homeless clients were not habitual drunkenness offenders (see table 4.11).

CONCLUSIONS

The Leeds system of taking in homeless men who were drunk in public produced a client group who were virtually all habitual drunkenness offenders, problem drinkers, and generally highly disadvantaged in terms of social, economic and medical criteria. One-third were chronic homeless. Besides these clients, there were others only admitted once, of whom little trace could be found in either court records of drunkenness offences or in the records of facilities for homeless men. It must be concluded that this group were different from typical Leeds referrals. However, at the other extreme were clients with very many admissions.

In the first three years of the Leeds experiment, 11 clients had 30 or more admissions. Data were available on eight of them who were admitted during the 15-week interviewing period. Nothing could be found which clearly distinguished them from the rest of the population. All eight had over 10 drunkenness convictions, but then so did 60 per cent of all Leeds admissions. Their alcohol dependence score

Table 4.11 Relationship between habitual drunkenness offending and homelessness across the centres

Centre	HDOs who were not homeless		Homeless HDOs		Homeless who were not HDOs		Neither homeless nor HDO
	No.	%	No.	%	No.	%	%
Leeds	24	35.0	33	49.0	8	12.0	4.0
Manchester	22	21.0	38	36.0	20	20.0	24.0
Tower Hamlets	6	7.0	38	46.0	24	31.0	17.0
Oxford	5	6.0	15	19.0	5	6.0	68.0
Portsmouth	5	10.0	4	8.0	4	8.0	73.0

was slightly above average (39 compared to 36.1), but half were not chronically homeless.

It would probably be mistaken to search for an explanation in terms of characteristics, when repeating was actually a result of *patterns of behaviour* – on the part of clients, police and detoxification centre staff.

The pattern at Manchester could not easily be typified, since it had the most varied admission procedures. Its client population therefore contained less extreme proportions of the types of clients seen at the other three special centres. Most reported serious drinking problems, but only two-thirds of police referrals, and half of other referrals were habitual drunkenness offenders and less than a quarter of each were Skid Row types.

Tower Hamlets admitted even more homeless clients than Leeds, had the highest level of drinking problems and tended to admit clients in a crisis. However, only half were habitual drunkenness offenders.

The Oxford referral system produced a group whose *chronic* problems did not appear as high as at the other special centres. Their average dependence score was lower and only seven were chronic homeless. Only a quarter were habitual drunkenness offenders. Yet most withdrawal symptoms were recorded at Oxford, suggesting more acute problems with drink than elsewhere.

Lastly, Portsmouth contained even more extremes within its clientele because it was not a special detoxification centre at all. Three-quarters of its clients were neither homeless nor habitual drunkenness offenders. The general patterns of admission of persons with drink problems to a psychiatric hospital appeared to exclude these groups.

5
Special Issues

PATTERNS OF ADMISSION AND LENGTHS OF STAY

Introduction

In the introductory chapter the lack of clarity in defining the word 'detoxification' has been highlighted; in the later chapters the lack of uniformity amongst detoxification services has been discussed. This chapter further highlights these differences. Although it is to be expected that there would be some differences in the number of people admitted to each of the centres, over a given period of time there is no immediate reason to expect great variations in the number of admissions these clients would make. However, it was felt that any variations that might occur could possibly be explained by referral sources, e.g. police versus non-police referrals.

Comparisons of the admissions data across the various detoxification centres was problematic since all the centres opened at different times: Leeds in May 1976 and Manchester in October 1977; the other two special centres had been operating for some while before Leeds opened; and St James' Hospital in Portsmouth had obviously been operating for many years.

It seemed appropriate to study the admissions patterns in the designated centres over each of their official three-year experimental periods. For the purposes of comparison, three-year periods of admission data were also studied at the other two special centres, over the same calendar period as the Manchester data. At Portsmouth all that could be collected were overall admission patterns, and the number of alcohol-related diagnoses involved. As this did not provide a precise enough guide to the number of people admitted who required detoxification treatment, this data is not presented. This section considers the patterns of admissions in the specialist centres, over the dates as shown in table 5.1.

Overall patterns of admission

Table 5.2 shows the number of clients admitted and the total number of admissions made in each individual year period, and the totals over the three-year periods.

A most noticeable feature is the general similarity in numbers of

Table 5.1   Dates of periods of study for each centre

	Total 3-Year Period		
	Year 1	Year 2	Year 3
Leeds	May 76–Apr 77	May 77–Apr 78	May 78–Apr 79
Manchester	Oct 77–Sept 78	Oct 78–Sept 79	Oct 79–Sept 80
Tower Hamlets	Oct 77–Sept 78	Oct 78–Sept 79	Oct 79–Sept 80
Oxford	Oct 77–Sept 78	Oct 78–Sept 79	Oct 79–Sept 80

Table 5.2   Summary of number of clients and number of admissions

		Leeds	Manchester	Tower Hamlets	Oxford
Year 1	No. of clients admitted	295	235	275	269
	No. of admissions	748	349	291	367
			(Police 345)		
Year 2	No. of clients admitted	377	358	323	316
	No. of admissions	1,101	516	336	400
			(Police 449)		
Year 3	No. of clients admitted	303	391	352	386
	No. of admissions	816	523	363	518
			(Police 303)		
Total 3-year period	No. of clients admitted	825	810	874	818
	No. of admissions	2,665	1,388	990	1,285
			(Police 1,097)		

clients admitted. However, clients in Leeds tended to make a greater number of repeat admissions than clients elsewhere.

Interestingly, in both the designated centres the number of police referrals increased in their second experimental year, as would be expected, but fell away again in their third year. Conversely, admissions to Oxford, Tower Hamlets and non-police referrals in Manchester gradually increased each year. At Manchester this perhaps could be explained in terms of the introduction of non-police referrals after the centre had been open for some time. But the biggest rises were in Oxford which admitted 43 per cent more clients in their third recorded year than in their first. Tower Hamlets also admitted similar numbers of clients, and as has been seen in chapter 4, they were somewhat similar to the Leeds clients in terms of homelessness, and recorded the highest score anywhere of dependence on alcohol. Surprisingly, they showed the lowest incidence of repeated admissions of any of the specialist centres. Repeat visits were made only very occasionally. At Tower Hamlets – over the three-year period – only 102 clients were admitted three times. No one was admitted to Tower Hamlets more than three times within the three-year period. This can partly be explained by their policy, which looked for motivation for rehabilitation amongst clients, and naturally this augured against clients who had already been in previously. It would also appear from the study that the clients increasingly moved out of the centre's immediate catchment area.

Table 5.3 shows the average number of admissions per client for each centre over the individual year periods and the total period. The proportion of repeating at each centre was fairly stable over each of their three years. As has already been discussed, Tower Hamlets had hardly any re-admissions, Manchester and Oxford had a greater incidence of repeating but Leeds had the greatest number with the average being more than twice that of Tower Hamlets. The average for the total three years at Leeds is higher than those of the individual years because the majority of repeating had been conducted by

Table 5.3   Average admissions per client

	Leeds	Manchester	Tower Hamlets	Oxford
Year 1	2.5	1.5	1.1	1.4
Year 2	2.9	1.4	1.0	1.3
Year 3	2.7	1.3	1.0	1.3
TOTAL	3.2	1.7	1.1	1.6

relatively few clients, who each made a large number of visits. At the other three centres the opposite pattern emerged. Therefore the averages for the whole three-year period were not much higher than for the individual periods. The patterns of repeating were obviously very different. At Tower Hamlets, repeating only happened very rarely while progressively more repeating occurred at Oxford, Manchester and Leeds.

However, at Leeds, the number of individual repeaters, and the number of admissions which they made, were vastly in excess of those at the other centres. Twenty-one men (3 per cent) were admitted over 20 times, and six men over 40 times. One man had been admitted 79 times over the three-year period.

This massive degree of repeating was thought to merit a special study and it presented a unique opportunity to observe individual's admission 'careers', their relationships to length of stay and possibly to outcome. Although problem drinking is characterised by chronic relapse, no other centre (or other types of specialist agencies) permit continuing access to treatment, after repeated use, especially over short periods of time.

Patterns of centre use in Leeds

For this sub-study of admissions patterns and associated behaviour at the Leeds centre, the analysis concentrated on all individuals whose first admission to the centre occurred within the first 140 days of the centre being opened, the period from 1 May 1976 to 17 September 1976. There were 136 persons admitted during this period; the admission patterns for each of these were traced over four successive periods of 180 days each subsequent to each individual's date of first admission. In the following analysis, T1 refers to the individual's first 180 day period following his first admission, T2 refers to the second 180 day period in each client's career of detox admissions, similarly for T3 and T4.

Of the 136 men who were admitted during the first 140 days and whose admissions were traced for the following two years, 51 (37.5 per cent) were admitted once and never again for at least two years. These men are referred to in the analysis as 'one-offs'.

The other extreme, eight chronic repeaters, were also admitted during the first 140 days. An analysis of their two-year careers showed that all eight shared a common characteristic in their pattern of visits. This was that they each had a greater number of admissions in T2 or T3 than in T1. That is, their number of visits, their tendency to repeat, *accelerated* over the first 12 to 18 months of their career.

Upon investigation a further 21 clients admitted during the first 140 days showed a similar pattern, and thus it appeared that they would eventually amass a large number of admissions. This gave a total number of 29 *'accelerators'* (21.3 per cent). Twenty-one of these 29 had made over 10 admissions in the first two years. The other eight accelerators made less than 10 visits over their individual two-year careers, but it was interesting to note that an accelerating number of visits over the second and third six months of the detox career could possibly predict the potential to become a very high repeater. For example, one of these eight had only a single admission in his first six months, two in his second six months, and then only single visits in each of his third and fourth six-month periods. This therefore classified him as an accelerator since the number of visits in T2 was greater than in T1. Yet this classification, even on the grounds of such a small number of visits, was later confirmed when his pattern of admissions after the end of the study period were investigated. More recently, following his loss of Part III accommodation, this resident began to accelerate the number of admissions in contrast with the majority of detox clients. It seems that even a slight period of acceleration, however small, indicates a potential to become a high visit repeater when combined with certain other circumstances. Thus the majority of high visit people had an accelerating number of visits in T2 or T3. This characteristic differentiated these residents from all the rest.

The majority of residents' careers were geared towards disappearance from the system, sooner or later, at least within the time period studied. If 'one-offs' were included in this pattern, then virtually four-fifths of clients admitted to the detox followed a decelerating pattern of visits. That is that they had more visits in T1 than in either T2 or T3. In fact the vast majority of them had all or nearly all of their visits in their T1, the period of six months following their first admission.

Irrespective of variations in lengths of stay or number of visits, clients with the highest proportion of visits closest to their first admission date can all be considered as decelerators. Just over half the residents admitted in the first 140 days were only admitted in their T1 and not again during the subsequent 18 months. A further 12 (9 per cent) were only seen within a period of one year, and 10 (7 per cent) were only seen over a period of 18 months. There were in fact only 31 residents (23 per cent) out of the 136 who made an appearance after 18 months, and only 15 (11 per cent) who were actually seen in every one of their four six-month periods. Therefore, in the majority of the cases the centre did not become a continual revolving door.

Changes in the proportions of types of detox users admitted over time

Since the distinction between types of detox user became evident within 18 months of their first admission date, during which time clients either accelerated or decelerated visits over time, it was there-

Table 5.4   Types of detox user admitted over two periods of time to the Leeds centre

| | Types of detox user admitted during | | | |
| | first 140 days | | first 320 days | |
	N	%	N	%
Accelerating repeaters	29	21.3	40	14.8
Decelerating repeaters	56	41.2	101	37.4
One-offs	51	37.5	129	47.8
TOTAL	136		270	

fore possible to extend the analysis from the 136 clients admitted during the first 140 days to clients admitted during the first 320 days. Two hundred and seventy individual clients made their first appearance at the detox during this period, and their admission careers were traced over the 18 months subsequent to each individual's first date of admission.

By the time the detox had been open for 320 days, nearly half of all clients admitted were not seen again within 18 months of their admission. As more individuals were admitted, the proportion of accelerating repeaters amongst them declined. Twenty-nine accelerators were admitted during the first 140 days of detox operation, and only a further 11 were admitted during the following 180 days.

Table 5.4 shows the proportion of accelerating repeaters, decelerating repeaters and one-offs who were admitted during both the first 140 days and the first 320 days. There is a decrease in the proportion of accelerators, the more chronic type of repeaters; the reasons for this are discussed later.

Types of centre user: the relationship between visit patterns and lengths of stay

For the purposes of this analysis, length of stay was divided into two categories – short stay and long stay. Since the envisaged stay of detox clients in Leeds was 10 days, 'short stay' was taken as a stay of less than five days, while 'long stay' was taken as a period of five days or more. In practice, it was found that during this period only a small number of residents in any group ever stopped between three and eight days. Thus in most cases 'short stay' implied a stay of less than three days, and 'long stay' one of eight days or more.

It was also found that classifying persons who made more than one admission as short stay or long stay according to their mean length of stay, in each six-month period, was not significantly different from classifying them according to the length of stay of the majority of their visits. Thus the mean length of stay per six-month period was a reasonable representation of the person's overall pattern of stay. This was because most decelerators consistently made visits of similar lengths. All their visits would be of less than five days, or all would be of more than five days. The various combinations of mean short and long stay with visit patterns were as follows.

One-offs

Table 5.5 shows the lengths of stay of all the 144 persons who were admitted once during the first year the detox was open and who were not admitted again. The majority of them, 62.5 per cent, stopped less than 36 hours. However, those who stayed longer than 36 hours tended to stop for a long period. In fact a quarter of one-offs stayed for nine days or more. Only 10 per cent therefore stayed between 1½ and 9½ days.

Table 5.5 Length of stay of clients admitted to the Leeds centre

		N	%	N	%
Very short	0.5 days or less	38	26	90	63
stay	0.5 to 1.5 days	52	36		
Medium	1.5 to 4.5 days	5	3	15	10
stay	4.5 to 9.5 days	10	7		
Long stay	9.5 to 10.5 days	28	19	39	27
	10.5 days or more	11	8		
TOTAL		144		144	

One-off short stayers   Interestingly, nearly a third (31.9 per cent) of the men admitted during this period stayed for less than 36 hours. Naturally, there was not much information available on these people, but there was good reason to believe that a proportion of these men did not fit strictly into the target population of the detox centre. Some were known to be employed, to live with relatives and/or not have a serious drinking problem.

One-off long stayers   This group were invariably single men with a drinking problem; all but two of the 40 men in this category were aged over 35. Most of these men lived in facilities for the homeless and rootless such as Shaftesbury House, Salvation Army hostels and commercial lodging-houses, but appeared to be relatively settled in this accommodation.

These men therefore did come within the target population, but were perhaps relatively more settled than men with more than one admission. After their first visit, 34 (85 per cent) of the 40 were discharged to arranged accommodation, and as far as could be ascertained from the files, they often returned after their stay to the same accommodation they had been using when they were apprehended.

Decelerators

The various patterns of numbers of visit and lengths of stay amongst decelerating repeaters (13.3 per cent) of the first 270 clients were really all variations around the central theme of decline and drop out from the detox population. Within this population of decelerators there was found to be a considerable consistency of relationships between numbers of visits and lengths of stay. Most clients in this group who made less than five visits were found to stay about the same length of time on each occasion. Decelerators who made five visits or more, however, tended to either gradually increase or decrease their mean length of stay as their detox career progressed.

Low visit decelerators   For the purpose of the analysis, a low visit resident was defined as someone who made two, three or four visits over a two-year career following his first admission. In virtually every case for persons in this group subsequent admissions followed closely on their first admission. Low visit residents fell into two distinct groups:

Low visit short stayers   Twenty-four persons admitted in the first 320 days, only 9 per cent of all admissions, made between two and four visits each lasting less than five days. These were usually all made within the first six months of admission. Virtually all these residents only managed to accumulate a total length of stay of five days throughout their detox career. Not surprisingly, a sample study of 12 of these 24 (selected by eliminating every alternate admission) was unable to produce much information about these short stayers. This is only to be expected since hardly any of them had spent more than a total of five days in the detox.

It appeared that low visit short stayers resembled one-off short stayers: the short stay on each of their visits demonstrating that they had no wish to remain in the detox.

Low visit long stayers   Just as low visit short stayers appeared to be like one-off short stayers, so low visit long stayers appeared similar to one-off long stayers. These 30 residents (11 per cent) admitted during the first 320 days made between two and four visits usually all within the six-month period following their first admission. All of

these visits were usually of nine days or more, and these residents accumulated a total of 21 or 22 days in their detox career.

With these men again it looked as though they tended to be relatively settled, but were prone for a period of time to be arrested for being publicly drunk. They used their stay in the detox to the full extent, building themselves up for their return to some form of relatively stable accommodation.

Other low visit decelerators Apart from the consistent groupings outlined above of low visit residents, there were just a few residents who did not fit into these groups. This remainder of low visit decelerators, 11 residents (4 per cent), admitted during the first 320 days, made one very short visit and one very long visit over their 18-month career. As yet it has not been possible to explain this pattern of two random visits, and as a group they appeared to have no particular distinguishing characteristics.

High visit decelerators High visit clients are defined as those who made five or more visits over a two-year career. High visit decelerators resembled low visit clients in that they crammed most of their admissions into a six-month period following their first admission, after which their visits fell away and eventually they disappeared from the detox altogether. Thirty-six (13.3 per cent) of those first admitted during the first 320 days made at least five visits and followed careers of this type. Unlike the low visit decelerators whose length of stay remained consistent over their career, high visit decelerators changed and tended to exhibit a shift in their mean length of stay. Their length of stay either tended to consistently increase or to consistently decrease towards the end of their career. Although there is a lack of definitive evidence, there are indications that a decelerating pattern of repeated admissions, in which length of stay increased, was linked to a growing tendency of the client during that period to become more stable, and to be more likely to move to long-term treatment and rehabilitation. Whatever the case, decelerating repeaters appeared to be the most interesting group of all, in that they were the only group to exhibit a consistent change in their pattern of detox admission over time.

Accelerators
Accelerators were either chronic repeaters or else persons with the potential to become chronic repeaters. A pattern of an accelerating number of admissions over the first year to 18 months of a person's career in the detox unit indicated the likelihood that they would repeatedly use the detox, possibly as a revolving door, and had the potential to accrue a very large number of visits. They were formally distinguished in the analysis by the fact that they had more visits in either the second or third six months of their career than in the first

six months. This differentiated them from all other types of detox user. All other clients – 85 per cent of those admitted during the first 320 days – either made most of their visits within six months of their first admission or else they only ever made one admission.

Accelerators who only made five to nine visits over their two-year career were largely similar in their careers to high visit decelerators in that same range of number of visits. They stopped four to eight days on average and accumulated 30 to 50 days overall. However, whereas the repeating of high visit decelerators declined over a year to 18 months, the accelerators, even those who made less than five visits, exhibited no sign of dropping out of the detox catchment population. Moreover, if certain circumstances applied, then low visit accelerators would begin to rapidly make more visits. Accelerators increased their visits over 12 to 18 months and then were repeatedly admitted. They may have made less or more visits for a while in successive periods, their lengths of stay could shorten or lengthen abruptly, but whatever happened they kept on being admitted, unless they were taken out of the system.

Comment

From this analysis it was found that all chronic repeaters accelerate their admissions in the second and third six months of their detox career. These 'accelerators' – 15 per cent of detox clients – were chronic repeaters or persons with the potential to become chronic repeaters. Eight of the accelerators (3 per cent) were chronic repeaters who made at least 35 admissions. These eight clients accounted for 19 per cent of all admissions in the first two years of detox operation.

Another 13 per cent of centre clients were repeaters who made at least five visits within 18-month careers, but their admissions decelerated: most of their visits occurred within six months of their first admission and then fell away or stopped altogether. These 'decelerators' either gradually decreased or increased their length of stay as their career progressed. They were the only group to exhibit a consistent shift in their pattern of centre use, and decelerating repeat visits coupled with increasing mean length of stay appeared related to stabilisation and/or movement to hostels or Alcoholism Treatment Units.

The majority of detox clients (75 per cent) were admitted less than five times, and 48 per cent were only admitted once.

Over time, the proportion of one-off admissions increased and the proportion of accelerators decreased, suggesting that long-term repeaters were a small fixed population who were mostly admitted soon after the centre opening.

Because the core repeat group accelerated admission over time, the problem of repeating appeared to the staff to be getting worse, whilst the proportion of individual accelerators was actually dropping. Furthermore, decelerating repeaters with lengthening stay were sometimes seen as 'worse' repeaters because they were resident for longer periods; whereas it could have been related to increasing motivation to attempt sobriety.

Sixty-three per cent of one-off admissions stopped less than 36 hours. Some of these did not fit admission criteria, e.g. they were not of no fixed abode. Police may have brought such men by mistake or because the referral system was easier for them to operate than taking men to the cells or casualty departments. Most of the other one-offs stopped nine days or more. Along with 11 per cent of detox clients who made two, three or four long visits, one-off long stayers fitted admission criteria and lived in facilities for single homeless, but possibly in a relatively settled way. For such clients admission may have prevented loss of accommodation which arrest or imprisonment for non-payment could have caused.

Lengths of stay throughout the study period

The pattern of lengths of stay in the specialist centres fell into two broad types. At the designated centres, high proportions left very quickly and high proportions stayed more than ten days with the rest of admissions being distributed evenly between 2 and 10 days. Table 5.6 shows these percentages over the total three-year period studied.

At Tower Hamlets and Oxford, most clients stopped a number of days roughly concordant with their projected programmes: between three and seven days at Oxford, and five and eight days at Tower Hamlets.

Each centre's pattern developed over the three years of study. It has already been noted that peak activity of police referrals to the

Table 5.6 Lengths of stay at the Leeds and Manchester centres

Lengths of stay	Number of admissions			
	Leeds		Manchester	
	N	%	N	%
1 day or less	1,194	45	559	40
2–10 days	727	27	522	38
More than 10 days	744	28	307	22

designated centres occurred within their second experimental year. At Leeds this increase in admissions was also accompanied by a large number of clients stopping for the whole 10-day programme and longer, whilst the proportion of early leavers decreased.

The cumulative effect was an apparent large increase in the total number of 'days' the centre was occupied. This does not mean the centre was running well below capacity in its first and third years, since 'days' of occupancy at Leeds was not the same thing as bed occupancy. Besides the detox beds there were also after-care beds which could, in times of need, have been used for clients within the detoxification programme proper. Moreover, at any one time, Leeds could have on its premises more clients than it had beds, since clients upon admission were kept in a holding room, often for a number of hours. During the monitoring of admission processes in Leeds it was found that 59 per cent of admissions were detained in the holding room at least 7 hours, and on occasions more than 16 hours. This should be borne in mind when considering the Leeds data.

Early leaving

Both designated centres were affected by high numbers of admissions leaving soon after their arrival (see table 5.7). More than a third of all admissions in all three periods in both designated centres stopped only one day or less. This phenomenon decreased in Leeds during the second experimental year but then increased considerably to 56 per cent in the third. In Manchester, early leaving was at its highest, and higher than at Leeds, during the second year. However, as the influence of accepting planned referrals as well as police referrals and the decrease in actual number of police referrals began to take effect in the third year, this proportion dropped to 35 per cent. In effect, Manchester in its third year began to move slightly towards the pattern exhibited at those centres which were not

Table 5.7   Number of clients at four centres leaving within one day or less

	Leeds		Manchester		Tower Hamlets		Oxford	
	No.	%	No.	%	No.	%	No.	%
Year 1	332	43	136	39	28	10	53	14
Year 2	398	36	242	47	29	9	38	10
Year 3	474	58	181	35	24	7	43	8

designed to take police referrals; at Tower Hamlets and Oxford only between 7 per cent and 14 per cent in any year left after one day or less. This difference between designated and non-designated centres basically reflected the difference between centres which accepted unpredictable police referrals of drunkenness offenders versus those whose admissions were usually arranged in advance. Although Oxford took in clients with acute withdrawal problems, 87 per cent of admissions arrived at a pre-arranged time. Leeds and Manchester could not determine whom the police brought, what precise condition they would be in or when they would arrive. Clients had not, at least in most cases, 'decided' or wanted to go to the detoxification centre. Although clients were given a choice as to whether they would prefer to be admitted to the centre rather than be charged – upon waking, sobering up or otherwise realising that they could leave the centre – a large proportion of clients left immediately.

Long length of stay

Yet in contrast to this, designated centres were also more concerned with influencing clients whilst resident within the centre towards longer-term treatment and rehabilitation. Whilst Tower Hamlets and Oxford were geared towards dealing primarily with clients' acute problems and referring them on for chronic problems of drinking and homelessness, Leeds and Manchester saw themselves as beginning the process of rehabilitation, etc. within the detoxification centre itself. Accordingly, lengthy stays were also more common at the designated centres than at Oxford and Tower Hamlets (see table 5.8).

Set against the high levels of repeating and early leaving at Leeds must be placed the finding that during the first year, a third of all admissions resulted in the client staying the full 10-day programme and longer, whilst in the second year this increased to 44 per

Table 5.8 Number of clients at four centres staying 10 days or more

	Leeds		Manchester		Tower Hamlets		Oxford	
	No.	%	No.	%	No.	%	No.	%
Year 1	241	32	98	29	24	8	7	2
Year 2	484	44	124	24	26	8	7	2
Year 3	116	27	156	30	25	7	11	2

cent. Even in the third year when admissions fell away, 27 per cent still remained for the full programme. Manchester again exhibited a fall in long-staying in the second year to accompany the increase in that year of early leaving, but the situation improved in the third year.

It was most unusual for anyone at Oxford to stop so many days. A mere 2 per cent in any period stopped 10 days or more. At Tower Hamlets, between 11 per cent and 15 per cent in any period stopped nine days or more, but although they catered largely for homeless clients, only 4 per cent in the first year studied remained there more than 10 days, and this went down to 2 per cent in the subsequent years. Of course the programmes at Tower Hamlets and Oxford were primarily geared to alleviation of immediate problems and were not intended to last as long as 10 days. Moreover neither Tower Hamlets nor Oxford were too afflicted by recurrent early leaving. At Tower Hamlets no more than 9 per cent in any period left after one day or less. During the first year over half (54 per cent) stopped between 5 and 8 days inclusive. In the second year this proportion became concentrated within 6 to 8 days (52 per cent) with more concentration still in the third year on a stay of 6 to 7 days (45 per cent).

At Oxford, admissions during the first year of study were evenly distributed across stays of between 1 and 6 days (86 per cent) with particular concentration on stays of 3 or 4 days (38 per cent). Only 3 per cent stayed less than a day, and only 1 per cent in any of the periods studied stayed more than 10 days. In the subsequent two years, average length of stay gradually increased, from 4.1 days in year 1, to 4.5 days and then 4.8 days in year 3. In these years 10 per cent and 8 per cent respectively were early leavers, departing within a day or less.

Quite clearly, the ability of the two non-designated centres to control whom they admitted and when meant that most clients admitted stayed for a length of time appropriate to each centre's programme. However as the designated centres were unable to control whom the police brought, when they brought them or how many times they brought them, at least a third of all admissions in any period left very quickly. However these centres managed to keep many referrals for their full 10-day programmes and in some instances for considerably longer. At least 24 per cent of all admissions stopped 10 days or more in any period at both centres, and in Leeds's second year more admissions stopped the full programme than left after one day.

Summary

The different patterns of admission and lengths of stay were studied for the two designated centres and for the other two special centres,

Tower Hamlets and Oxford, over a three-year period. Since Portsmouth had no special centre, the information available could not provide a guide to the number of people admitted who required detoxification, therefore treatment details of admissions to Portsmouth were not considered appropriate and were thus not included here.

The annual number of clients admitted in the four centres was similar, but individual clients in Leeds tended to accumulate a greater frequency of repeated admissions than in any of the other centres; a special sub-study was therefore conducted of repeat admission there. Tower Hamlets had the lowest incidence of clients repeating. Repeat visits were made only very occasionally. This was partly due to their policy, which looked for motivation for rehabilitation amongst clients, and naturally this did not favour clients who had been admitted previously. The proportion of repeating in each centre was fairly stable over each of their three years. It was noted that despite the high number of repeated admissions made in Leeds, a vast bulk of repeating had been conducted by relatively few clients who made a large number of visits, some of whom subsequently went on to a rehabilitation hostel or treatment unit. At the three other centres there was a lesser number of repeat visits but these were more evenly distributed amongst the clients.

The patterns of lengths of stay fell into two broad types. At the designated centres, high proportions left very quickly and high proportions stayed more than 10 days (the length of the treatment programme). At the two non-designated centres, most clients stopped a number of days roughly concordant with their projected programmes. This difference between the designated centres basically reflected the differences between centres which accepted unpredictable police referrals of drunkenness offenders versus those whose admissions were usually prearranged. Leeds and Manchester could not determine whom the police brought, what precise conditions they would be in or when they would arrive. Despite this the designated centres were more concerned with influencing clients whilst resident within the centre towards rehabilitation. While Tower Hamlets and Oxford were geared towards dealing primarily with clients' acute problems and referring them on for chronic problems of drinking and homelessness, Leeds and Manchester saw themselves as beginning the process of rehabilitation within the detoxification centre itself.

Conclusions

There are considerable differences across the centres in the numbers of clients admitted over similar periods of time and it seems that these differences can to a certain extent be explained by the different referral sources and criteria for admission to the centres.

The more concentrated study in Leeds shows that clients' behaviour can, to a certain extent, be predicted by their lengths of stay and frequency of admission. It also shows that only for a handful of clients do the experimental detox centres become part of a revolving door system. This should cause policy makers to question criticisms that have been suggested that repeated admissions are a sign of failure on the part of the service to 'cure' problem drinkers. It perhaps goes further to indicate that sobriety as a measure of 'success' is a rather stringent requirement, and any evaluation of success should consider the degree of impact on an individual's behaviour over time. In this respect, drink-related problems are no different from medical ailments in that they can require repeated treatment before a patient can be considered as being 'cured'.

APPREHENSION AND DIVERSION OF HABITUAL DRUNKENNESS OFFENDERS

Since the nineteenth century it has been argued that public drunkenness offenders should be removed from the penal system and directed instead into health and social welfare agencies.

The view held by the Weiler committee (1971) was that 'so far as treatment is concerned, criminal and penal processes have proved inadequate as a remedy both for society and for the individual' (1.4). Following experiments with detoxification centres in Eastern Europe and North America, the Weiler Report recommended the establishment of experimental centres to which the police could take drunkenness offenders instead of processing them through the courts.

The designated centres in Leeds and Manchester were set up in response to these recommendations; there have also been changes in legislation designed to keep drunkenness offenders out of prison. Detoxification centres have been the most popular proposal for the decriminalisation of public drunkenness and in his review of the literature, Orford stated that 'for evaluation purposes the question may reasonably be asked, do detoxification centres result in diversion on a significant scale?' (p. 5). Various aspects of diversion were considered during the research on detoxification centres:

Apprehension

The process of apprehension was studied at Leeds in 1977. By then, a number of teething troubles with the original admission criteria and referral procedure had been resolved. It was agreed that the centre would accept men who were: arrested for being either drunk and incapable or drunk and disorderly within three specific police divisions, who were of no fixed address or who gave the address of accommodation known to be for the homeless. However, men fulfilling these criteria would not be admitted to the centre if they urgently required medical attention, if they had been arrested for committing another offence besides drunkenness or if they were wanted on a warrant for a previous offence.

The centre obviously could not accept admissions if it was already full. At such times, the centre informed officers in the police information room who in turn would inform officers on duty within the catchment area. Occasionally, the centre decided temporarily to refuse entry to a man because it was felt, for various reasons, that admission would not be beneficial to him. If an arrested man refused to be admitted to the centre, s. 34 of the 1972 Criminal Justice Act permitted the police to then take him instead to the police station and charge him with the appropriate drunkenness offence. This rarely happened in Leeds, but the Manchester police reported it happened frequently there. This may have been because the police there were also offering the detoxification alternative to non-homeless offenders who may have preferred a court appearance to admission to a unit for 'alcoholics'.

In Leeds the process of apprehension was straightforward. Upon picking up a public drunk, the apprehending officer would ask him if he wished to be taken to the centre and if so the officer radioed the station to see if the man had any outstanding warrants and to check if there was a place at the centre. If there were no problems, they accompanied or transported him to the centre. The client would then be admitted unless he refused to enter or the nurse felt that he should go straight to hospital. The officer would not be required to search a man, and it was the centre staff's job to make a record of his property.

The study of apprehension at Leeds
A study was made of all admissions to the centre over a nine-week period. With the agreement of the community liaison officer, arresting officers completed a research form every time they brought a man to the centre. During this time 86 men were admitted to the detox, making a total of 146 admissions. Eighty-five per cent of the men admitted made only one or two admissions during this period.

Characteristics of apprehending officers
Apprehensions were made by 85 individual arresting officers, 68 (80 per cent) of whom made no more than two separate apprehensions. The majority of men were brought to the centre by the officer by whom they had been arrested (133, 91 per cent) and in the arresting officer's own vehicle (116, 79 per cent). Only 11 (8 per cent) of those arrested were taken via the police station to the centre.

Type of offence
Of the 146 apprehensions in this period, 140 (96 per cent) were
arrested for being drunk and incapable. Although the criteria of the
target population of the centre explicitly included homeless men
arrested for drunk and disorderly, only four (3 per cent) had been
apprehended for this offence. The proportion of drunk and disorderly being taken to the centre was much lower than would be
expected from a study of court records of drunkenness offences in
Leeds. This disinclination of arresting officers to bring drunk and
disorderly offenders to the centre had been discussed between the
centre staff and police at the end of 1976, and at that time it had been
thought erroneously that this problem had been resolved.

Time and place of apprehension
The peak time of apprehensions of centre clients was between 2 p.m.
and midnight, during which hours over three-quarters of admissions
arrived. The remaining arrests were evenly divided over other times.
About 70 per cent (109) of arrests were made on public thoroughfares, only 11.6 per cent (17) being in public parks or gardens.

Seventy-five per cent (82) of arrests in public thoroughfares took
place in one of a series of streets in the city centre and/or major public
thoroughfares.

The study of court records also showed that this same group of
streets figured prominently amongst the overall distribution of
drunken arrests in Leeds. Hence, the geographical distribution of
arrests of detox clients was the same as that of drunkenness offences
overall.

Length of time between apprehension and admission
In over half the apprehensions (75, 51.3 per cent) of the men arrested
were admitted to the centre less than five minutes after their arrest.
The centre was conveniently situated on a major road a mile from the
main pick-up area of homeless drunkenness offenders. In only five
cases (3.4 per cent) did it take the police more than half an hour to
admit a man to the centre.

Attitudes of the police to the centre and its clients

If a centre taking police referrals is to have any chance of success,
then the police must not just be willing to co-operate, but also be
involved in, and committed to, a partnership with the centre.
Clearly, the West Yorkshire Metropolitan Police Force were committed to the development of this partnership and the staff of the
centre in turn made considerable efforts to clarify their desired target
population and to encourage police involvement.

Thus, not only were the police involved in the planning of the
Leeds centre from the initial stages, but also priority was given to

ensuring that the procedure involved facilitated appropriate referrals and allowed the continuance of good working relations.

The liaison officer for the Leeds detox arranged for a pilot study of attitudes of two small samples of policemen, one in a police district serving the detoxification centre, and another in a comparable district outside the catchment area. A questionnaire was designed to measure the attitudes of the police in terms of:
• attitudes towards drunkenness offenders, homeless and home-based
• the reasons for arresting drunkenness offenders
• treatment, rehabilitation or punishment of drunkenness offenders
• attitudes towards specialist centres for homeless drunkenness offenders

The respondents in both groups tended to think that homeless drunkenness offenders could not change their behaviour, and disliked dealing with them because of their physical unpleasantness. Those outside the detox catchment area were more likely to view this client group as 'smelly' and 'infested'. However, neither group considered homeless drunks to be a particularly troublesome group, and indeed they thought they were less difficult than drunken drivers. Those amongst the police who believed that the homeless drunkenness offender could change also favoured the provision of facilities for them and did not see these as a waste of scarce resources. They thought that centres made their job easier. Those who most considered the picking up of homeless drunkenness offenders to be a waste of time were also those most repulsed by them.

Apart from views on the relative unpleasantness of drunkenness offenders, the findings suggest that the presence of a centre taking police referrals did not have any major influence on the attitudes of the police to the clients of the centre. However, there is some suggestion that perhaps the police in the centre catchment area, by having more contact with homeless drunkenness offenders, held slightly less stereotypical attitudes about their appearance.

It is perhaps more interesting that the police were prepared to use the centre frequently despite not seeing the homeless drunkenness offender in any more positive light. Clearly, the reasons for this are to do with other factors than police perception of this group and their needs.

Discussions with the police at Leeds and with staff of the centres at Leeds and Manchester suggest the following would influence the number of police referrals to centres:
• Location. The nearer a centre was to the relevant police districts and to the areas where homeless people congregate, the more likely would regular referral occur. Much of the success of the Leeds

system was simply due to its being so quick for the police to use. In Manchester the centre was situated some way from the city centre on a road which often experienced a build-up of traffic.

• Police procedure and apprehension. The same point pertains to straightforwardness of the procedures required of police on making an arrest. At Leeds a man could be brought directly to the centre, in the officers' car or van, or even on foot. All that was required was that the officer radioed the station to check whether there was a warrant out or not for the arrest of this person. In contrast, at Manchester it was necessary to send for a police van which had to service a number of police districts for various purposes, and at one stage the person apprehended had to be taken to the station before being taken to the centre.

• Paperwork. The ease of referral to the Leeds centre was facilitated by the small amount of paperwork required compared to making a charge. The officer did not have to attend court when the charge was being heard.

• The support of superiors and courts for the system. In Leeds the police were very actively encouraged by superior officers to use the system, and the community liaison officer was highly committed to the success of the scheme. In the courts, if a homeless man appeared on a drunkenness charge, magistrates would often enquire of the arresting officer why he had not been taken to the detoxification centre.

Drunkenness offences

One of the goals attributed to designated centres is the diversion of habitual drunkenness offenders from the penal system. Table 5.9 shows the numbers of findings of guilt for drunkenness in West Yorkshire and Greater Manchester from 1975 to 1980. The numbers of findings of guilt for drunkenness increased in the West Yorkshire area by 15 per cent from 1975 to 1980. Conversely, in Greater Manchester there was a decrease of 1.3 per cent. The increase in West Yorkshire is consistent with the national figures of a 14.6 per cent increase in these five years.

On the basis of these figures it would seem that the Manchester centre did affect the number of drunkenness offenders processed whereas the Leeds centre did not.

In interpreting these figures it is important to bear in mind that the catchment area for the Leeds centre was smaller than the catchment area for Manchester and covered fewer police districts. In fact, when the Leeds catchment area figures are considered, rather than the whole of West Yorkshire, the same phenomenon of a decrease in arrests appears to emerge.

Table 5.9 Findings of guilt for drunkenness in West Yorkshire and Greater Manchester, 1975–80

Drunkenness Offenders	1975	1976	1977	1978	1979	1980
West Yorkshire	4,620	4,626	4,545	5,018	5,437	5,495
Per cent increase per annum		0.1	−1.8	10.4	8.3	1.1
Greater Manchester	7,697	7,880	8,119	7,192	7,596	7,593
Per cent increase per annum		2.4	3.0	−11.4	5.6	0

NB The centre at Leeds opened in May 1976 and in Manchester in October 1977
Source: Home Office Statistics Division 1982

In 1976, when the detoxification centre opened, there were 2,894 offences. In the following year of continuous detoxification operation, there were only 2,485, and 2,534 in 1978. However, there had been several fluctuations in the Leeds rates throughout the previous years, and there had been almost as large decreases in 1972 and 1974. Indeed, the largest increase throughout the 1970s was in 1976, when the detoxification centre was open for seven months. Clearly, then, a more precise picture is needed.

The numbers of findings of guilt for drunkenness does not give a clear picture of the extent to which diversion of drunkenness offenders occurred.

In particular, the impact or otherwise of detoxification on the court appearances of the target group of habitual drunkenness offenders remains unknown. For this reason, it was decided in the present study to examine data on *individual* drunkenness offences in Leeds over a period of years. The situation in Leeds was more geographically concise than in Manchester and during its experimental period, the centre would *only* accept referrals of drunkenness offenders brought by the police. Therefore, a straightforward analysis of the extent of diversion from the penal system was possible. Moreover, liaison between this centre and the police force was particularly good, so that the potential for diversion could be measured at its optimum.

All drunkenness offences in the court records were collected for a period of three years from a date 12 months before the opening of the detoxification centre until a date 24 months after its opening – from May 1975 until April 1978 inclusive. As Orford (1982) has argued, ideally it would take some years longer than this to identify fully changes in patterns, but the task of collecting three years of data in this detail proved massive and time-consuming. In any case, the longer the period studied, the more these changes might be due to changes in interpretation of law, police policy and staffing, rather than the actual impact of a detoxification service. Thus studying a three-year period in great detail seemed a reasonable compromise.

The catchment area of the detoxification centre comprised three police divisions in and around the Leeds city centre. During the periods studied, drunkenness offenders were dealt with in specific courts on specific days of the week. Data on every drunkenness offence, therefore, was collected from the relevant courts on the relevant days. To ensure that the vast bulk of offences were being collected, a pilot study was made of the registers of each court on each day of the week for 12 separate weeks selected at random throughout the three-year study period. Virtually no drunkenness offenders were found to have slipped into the 'wrong' court.

Drunkenness offence rates before and after the opening of the detoxification centre
In each of the detoxification centres' first two years of operation, there were more offences in Leeds than there had been in the year before the detoxification centre opened (see table 5.10).

Table 5.10 Pattern of drunkenness offending in Leeds before and after opening of detox centre

	No. of individuals	No. of offences
Pre-detox year 75/76	1,806	2,513
Year 1 of detox	2,050	2,844
Year 2 of detox	1,971	2,653

The rise in offences is even more remarkable when considered with the numbers of detoxification admissions (all technically for drunkenness offences) (see table 5.11).

Table 5.11 Relationship between numbers of court appearances and detox centre admissions in Leeds, 1975–78

Year	Total court appearances	Total detoxification centre admissions	Total offences
1975	2,407	–	2,407
1976	2,894	468	3,362
1977	2,485	1,076	3,561
1978	2,534	994	3,528

If detoxification admissions are added to drunkenness offenders, the number of total drunkenness offences in Leeds in the calendar year in which the detoxification centre first opened was 40 per cent higher than it had been in the previous year. In 1977, the first full calendar year of detox operation, there were a remarkable 48 per cent more arrests than in 1975, the last full calendar year without a detoxification service.

Why a detoxification system might increase arrests for drunkenness
The above phenomenon of a detoxification centre *increasing* rather than *decreasing* the number of drunkenness arrests has been noted

elsewhere (Orford, 1982). In some areas of Ontario, for example, the total number of police arrests increased after the initiation of a detoxification service. This type of outcome is not so much an example of a system failing as rather highlighting a basic naivety in the theory of diversion via detoxification centres. It has been assumed in much of this literature and politicking that a person taken to a detoxification centre is automatically a person removed from the courts. The evidence from Leeds suggests that this is certainly not the case. Therefore simplistic cost-benefit 'justifications' for detoxification centres on the grounds of each admission representing a certain saving in police and court time and expense do not stand up to detailed examination of what actually happens when a detoxification centre opens its doors. As Annis (1979) has pointed out from the Canadian experience, evaluation is difficult because as soon as the new procedure begins, the policing operations and assumptions all change as well. Orford suggested, in his review of the literature, 'the process is highly complex and does not correspond to a simple diversion of drunkenness offenders from criminal justice to social and health care'. The Leeds data points to two major ways in which arrests increased:

1   The number of admissions to the detoxification centre made by repeating offenders was far in excess of the number of court appearances which they would have made had the detoxification centre not existed.

Consider, for example, the data on a Leeds client who was known to be resident in the city throughout most of the year prior to the detoxification centre opening, apart from two short spells in hospital. During the year before the detoxification centre opened he committed two drunkenness offences. Yet within two years of the detoxification centre opening, not only had the police taken him to the detoxification centre on 54 occasions, but he had also passed through the Leeds courts on charges of drunkenness offences on a further 27 occasions! Furthermore, there were another eight clients who had single figure court appearances in the year before the detoxification centre opening but who registered double figure appearances at *both* the detoxification centre and the Leeds courts in each of the first two years of detoxification operation.

2   The diversionary impact of the detoxification centre was made even more obscure because when the detoxification centre was running, the same individuals were on some occasions being taken to the centre and on other occasions to the courts. Two hundred and sixty-six individuals appeared in both the detoxification centre during its first two years, and also the Leeds courts at some point during that same period. One hundred and seventy-three of these had never appeared in the courts in the

year before the detox opening. In its most extreme form, three men had committed no offences at all in the year prior to detox, but then between them within two years totted up over a hundred detoxification centre admissions, coupled with over a hundred court appearances. While the detoxification centre was running, in the two-year study period, detoxification centre clients accounted for 17 per cent of all the Leeds court appearances (compared with 13 per cent in the year the detoxification centre opened).

There may have been fair reasons for this. Clients might have been arrested at a time when the detoxification centre happened to be full and thus were taken to the courts instead. Some clients who were admitted repeatedly to the centre were on occasions 'banned' from admission for short periods. However, these factors alone would not account for the large increases in arrests. Other more crucial elements should be considered:

Type of offence   It has already been noted that when men were arrested for being drunk and incapable, they were more likely to be sent to the detoxification centre than if they were drunk and disorderly. It should be stressed that in Leeds, the police were as positive as might be expected about working the detoxification system, but nevertheless, in interviews they felt that a person arrested for drunk and disorderly should really be punished and processed through the courts.

The trend towards segregating incapable and disorderly offenders can be traced in the court records. Nationally, drunkenness offences are usually split almost exactly half-way between incapable and disorderly offences. Sure enough, in Leeds, the year before the detoxification centre opened, they were virtually identical – 1,256 drunk and incapable offences and 1,255 drunk and disorderly offences. However, by the second year of detoxification operation, the number of drunk and incapable offences had decreased to 1,234 (46.5 per cent) whilst drunk and disorderly cases had risen to 1,409 (53.1 per cent). If the detoxification admissions were added to this, the trend would be even more marked, since it appears that most people taken to the detoxification centre were, in the view of the arresting officer, 'drunk and incapable'.

Age   There was a more evident shift amongst age groups, where – before the detoxification system commenced – a third of offences were committed by persons aged 46 and over. But this reduced to a quarter by the second year of detoxification operation, with corresponding rising proportions of court offences being committed by the younger groups, and particularly those aged 25 years or less. As can be seen from Table 5.12, in the second year of detoxification

Table 5.12   Age distribution of drunkenness offenders in Leeds before and after opening of detox centre

Age		under 26	26–35	36–45	46–55	56–65	over 65	DK	TOTAL
Year pre-detox 1975/76	No.	454	402	316	269	179	65	121	1,806
	%	25.1	22.3	17.5	14.9	9.9	3.6	6.7	
Year 1 of detox 1976/77	No.	647	458	367	245	167	44	122	2,050
	%	31.6	22.3	17.9	12.0	8.1	2.1	6.0	
Year 2 of detox 1977/78	No.	634	433	375	237	142	47	103	1,971
	%	32.2	22.0	19.0	12.0	7.2	2.4	5.2	

operation almost a third of drunkenness offences in Leeds were committed by those aged 25 years or less. This may even be another example of the detoxification system increasing arrests, in the sense that the partial decriminalisation of certain groups from the courts may have left more 'room' for disorderly young offenders who previously might have been just cautioned. Although the young group accounted for a high proportion of offences, their *rate* of offending was low, being 1.1 on average, whereas the older the group in the court data, the higher became their rate of offending. The reason for this was not that the police were taking pity on older offenders and transferring them to the detoxification centre, but rather the fact that repeat drunkenness offending was the norm amongst offenders aged over 65. The average offender in this age category committed two offences per year. The effect of the detoxification system was thus not to remove the number of older offenders from the courts, but rather to reduce their rates of appearances in the courts.

Patterns of offending It might be conjectured that since the detoxification centre was intended for *habitual* drunkenness offenders, these offenders, in particular, may have been siphoned off from the courts, leaving occasional offenders instead. However the data in table 5.13 shows that the proportion of habitual offenders in the Leeds courts did not change at all. A steady 7 per cent of offenders in each year were habitual offenders, and in each year they accounted for about 20 per cent of all offences. But the composition of the 7 per cent changed in an apparently paradoxical way. Before the detoxification centre opened, clients who were later admitted there comprised only 29 per cent of all the habitual drunkenness offenders in Leeds. In the years of detox operation studied, they increased to 43 per cent and then 49 per cent. That is, the longer the detoxification system continued, the higher the proportion of detoxification clients who also became habitual drunkenness offenders in the Leeds court! In the first and second years of detox operation, 102 men were arrested at least three times in Leeds inside each of those years but were *never* admitted to the detoxification centre in either of its first two years of operation. Since the detoxification centre was also intended for *homeless* habitual drunkenness offenders, it may be that these habitual drunkenness offenders within the courts did not fall within that population, but if this were the case, then serious questions would still be raised about the theory of diversion, since previously it has been assumed that most habitual drunkenness offenders must be homeless. It may be that the Leeds data suggests that this is not necessarily the case.

The geography of arrest The streets and sites of arrest were all noted from the court records. Despite the fact that most persons

Table 5.13   Patterns of drunkenness offending among detox users and non-users before and after opening of Leeds detox centre

	Non-habitual Offenders				Habitual Offenders			
	Detox users	Non-detox users	TOTAL		Detox users	Non-detox users	TOTAL	
			No.	%			No.	%
Year pre-detox 1975/76	61	1,415	1,476	82	35	86	121	7
Year 1 of detox 1976/77	81	1,570	1,651	81	64	84	148	7
Year 2 of detox 1977/78	84	1,525	1,609	82	66	68	134	7

taken to the detoxification centre were from one police district which covered most of the city centre, the bulk of people arrested and taken to court still came from the same main pick-up areas. The geography of drunkenness arrest patterns in Leeds remained virtually exactly the way it had been before.

Conclusions

The failure of diversion   The results of the study suggest that the Leeds experimental detox centre did not create a significant diversionary impact during its first two years of operation for the following reasons:

- the number of drunkenness offences and individual offenders in the Leeds court increased
- most habitual drunkenness offenders never went to the detoxification centre
- a large number of people who did go to the detoxification centre were not habitual drunkenness offenders
- large numbers of men appeared in *both* the detoxification centre and the court
- the demography and general pattern of drunkenness arrests in Leeds remained largely unaffected by the new system.

The complexities of diversion via detoxification   As stated previously, this apparent 'failure' of detoxification centres to divert, is equally a failure of theorists and planners. They did not foresee that the installation of a new system and process within their existing arrangements would create complexities of its own and could bring previously unconsidered phenomena to light.

The incidence of public drunkenness   One interpretation of the heavy repeating at the detoxification centre and the increase in offences when detoxification admissions are combined with court appearances, is that the incidence of public drunkenness might be far higher than is measured in official drunkenness statistics. It may also indicate that the homeless problem drinkers require more temporary help and shelter of a higher quality than was provided.

The incidence of help seeking   From interviews with clients in the Leeds detoxification centre it seemed that most of them liked being in the centre, or at least preferred it to the alternatives. Some of them clearly learnt how to 'play the system' and were able to gain entry to the detoxification centre by engineering their own arrest, such as by creating disturbances in places to which they knew the police would be called. The Leeds detoxification was clearly a very humane institution providing considerable sustenance to homeless men in Leeds. However, it is questionable how efficient or how appropriate is a system of help provision which requires a man to be humiliated by arrest by the police for drunkenness in order that he might receive that help.

Changes in police behaviour   On the whole, in a non-detoxification system, the police are unwilling to arrest persons who are quite clearly drunk in public. The police will often caution such people unless they are so incapable they might well injure themselves or others, or they have become very disorderly. The Weiler Report noted that 'our police witnesses left us in no doubt that dealing with drunkenness offenders made great demands on police time and resources, and was not an aspect of their work which they regarded as constructive'. Clearly the Leeds detoxification system changed that view amongst the police in Leeds. Instead of only arresting drunkenness offenders when they absolutely had to, the police began to pick up more drunks, because they were more aware of their difficulties, and because they felt a constructive alternative to arrest was available. When combined with the ease of operation for the police, it is not surprising that the number of arrests made by the police in Leeds should have increased so much. The Leeds experiment perhaps shows that given the chance to make a positive response and good liaison with a social and medical facility, the police were prepared and able to carry out a pick-up role.

The effect of the implementation of the 1967 Criminal Justice Act

Non-payment of fine for drunkenness
Section 91 (1) of the 1967 Criminal Justice Act took effect from 1 February 1978 (see appendix 1). This abolished immediate imprisonment for the offence of being drunk and disorderly and substituted a maximum penalty of £50 fine. It could be argued this was a form of decriminalisation. Offenders were no longer to be processed through prisons, only through the courts. Table 5.14 shows the number of persons imprisoned for drunkenness or in default of payment of fine for drunkenness between 1975 and 1980.

Table 5.14   Persons under sentence of immediate imprisonment in default of a payment of fine for drunkenness offences, 1975–80 (England and Wales)

	1975	1976	1977	1978	1979	1980
In default of payment of fine	4,291	4,256	2,270	2,683	3,074	2,529
Immediate imprisonment	423	360	427	27	–	–

The table indicates that there was an increase in numbers received into prison as fine defaulters in 1978 and 1979. In 1977 the total number of people received into prison for drunkenness offences was 427, whereas the number imprisoned for non-payment of fine between 1977 and 1978 was 391.

Figures were obtained from the Home Office Statistics Division on the number of fine defaulters received into prisons from courts at Leeds and Manchester. There was no significant change in the number of fine defaulters in Leeds after the centre opened. However, there was an increase of 22 per cent between 1976/77 and 1978/79, i.e. since the implementation of the Act. At Manchester there was a 51 per cent increase in the number of fine defaulters for the same period.

Admission to designated centres
Changes in the Criminal Justice Act implemented on 1 February 1978 were not found to have affected the numbers brought by police to the centre. There were virtually the same number of admissions (466) and the same number of individual people (198) admitted in the first 180 days of 1978 (1 January to 29 June 1978) as there had been in the first 180 days of 1977 (474/206).

As would be expected, the implementation of the Criminal Justice Act (s. 91) in February 1978 reduced the numbers immediately imprisoned for drunkenness but did not affect the numbers admitted to the centre at Leeds and may or may not have contributed to the numbers convicted and imprisoned for non-payment of a fine for drunkenness. The data from the Leeds and Manchester courts suggest that the implementation of the Act did affect the numbers imprisoned but the national figures do not confirm this. It may, however, be too early to tell since the prison officers strike in 1980 may have distorted or masked the implications of this change in the law.

Conclusions for policy

If Leeds is fairly typical of major English provincial cities, then if all habitual drunkenness offenders were removed from courts in all these areas, court loads *theoretically* would drop by about a fifth, although of course the number of individuals involved would drop less than that. But the Leeds experiment suggests that this amount of diversion would not *in actuality* occur, at least if the possibility remained that drunkenness offenders could also be taken to the courts or if the detoxification centre was unable at times to always accept them. A detoxification system such as in Leeds encouraged the police to arrest more people on more occasions than they would have done prior to detoxification operation, and at times it encouraged clients to get arrested. The net result was that the detoxification system came to operate *in addition* to the court system, *not instead of it*. Moreover it appears that there were a number of home-based habitual drunkenness offenders who remained unaffected by the system. Quite clearly, the question of how society should deal with habitual drunkenness offenders remains to be solved. But solved it should be, for other evidence from this study found that people who were habitual drunkenness offenders had a severe drinking problem. Thus it is pointless that this group should be processed and repeatedly punished by the courts: this is a waste of police and court time. However it may be that the type of detoxification system envisaged here too is not the best means of dealing with this problem. For although the Leeds detoxification was admirable in many ways and undoubtedly of benefit to its residents and the community in general in various ways, it clearly did not achieve a satisfactory diversion of habitual drunkenness offenders in Leeds from the penal system. Data has been presented from the other such experimental centre in Manchester that the opening of the detoxification centre coincided with a fall in drunkenness offences there. However, this study began by pointing out an apparent overall fall in Leeds, which disguised a quite different pattern underneath. Looking at overall patterns can obviously be deceptive. Although the drunkenness offence rate in Manchester had been rising in the 1970s, its rate of increase had been slowing in the two years before the detoxification centre opened. The number of both individuals and admissions brought to the Manchester centre by the police was nowhere as high as it was in Leeds, and given that the rate of drunkenness offending per head of population in Greater Manchester was usually about a third higher than in West Yorkshire, it is hard to believe that the Manchester detoxification experiment made much more diversionary impact than in Leeds. But if Manchester did have more effect on drunkenness rates, this would pose a 'Hobson's Choice' dilemma for planners of future centres. The Leeds centre, because of the ease of referral for the police, was often full and admitted a large number of people with immediate and chronic problems. However, this centre, because of the precise definition of its target population, and its over-use, could not significantly reduce the number of drunkenness offenders processed through the Leeds courts. Paradoxically, the centre at Manchester might have had more influence on the rates of drunkenness arrests because it was not as convenient for the police to use as the Leeds centre and therefore only obtained referrals of those who would definitely otherwise have been arrested. Yet ironically, because it was difficult to use, it could not achieve full occupancy via police referrals!

In spite of the problems in diverting the habitual drunkenness offender, pleas still have been made for further attempts to transfer all drunkenness offenders en bloc to detoxification centres or similar institutions such as 'wet shelters'. The Leeds court data would question the wisdom of such a move. If a relatively expensive institution with a high level of staffing and a very co-operative and positive police force was unable to make a significant impact on habitual drunkenness, it is uncertain what chance institutions might have which were less well-funded and supported. Moreover, during the three-year study period, a total of 3,974 individuals were arrested and appeared in the Leeds courts only once (these constituted 77.6 per cent); 3,867 of these individuals never went to the detoxification centre. Perhaps their re-appearance in the courts indicated that the experience of arrest and punishment did prevent it happening again. Can it be argued assuredly that it would have been to the benefit of these individuals or to society at large had they received a medical or social response instead?

CENTRE STAFFING, MORALE AND MANAGEMENT

The core functions of a centre, as outlined in chapter 2, are the management of intoxification and detoxification and where appropriate, the referring on of individuals for further help with short- and long-term problems. Although all of the centres performed these functions, the background and experience of the staff responsible for carrying them out varied, in some cases significantly; for example, the ratio of care assistants to nursing staff was unusual by comparison elsewhere. This variety in the use of staff rather suggests that there may be greater flexibility than first might be supposed as to the roles and tasks of those working in a centre.

However there are also common features. Nurses with experience in psychiatric care formed the basis of the staff teams in all the centres; no other professional groups were so consistently represented or so central to the staffing of the centres. The importance of psychiatric trained nurses to the effective functioning of a centre was highlighted by Hamilton (1976, 1977, 1979) who reported that a general poisons ward was less conducive than a special ward in a psychiatric hospital where the nurses were familiar with managing disturbed and difficult patients.

Given that the centres share similar functions, the staff thereof face, potentially, the same stresses and demands as well as opportunity for job satisfaction. The impact of these on individual staff and the performance of the staff team must depend to a large degree on the effectiveness of their management structure in providing support, supervision and opportunities for development; particularly where less experienced staff, such as care assistants, have a high level of responsibility. The centres varied considerably in terms of management structure, and yet shared a common commitment to multi-disciplinary team work.

Finally, it also seems worth noting that in all the centres the focus of resources had come to be the provision of staff (and the development of more services) as opposed to medical technology. This observation is consistent with the centres' role being perceived as primarily helping people with acute and chronic emotional and social difficulties and less so with acute physical problems.

Centre organisation and management

One of the crucial components in determining the way in which a centre functions is its staffing. Who they are, what they do, how they do it, their experience, expertise, the resources available to them and their attitudes to their work are all features of the organisation of a centre that can determine how effective a service can be and for whom. It was therefore thought to be important to describe and compare the nature of the centres' staffing and management in the light of each centre's particular style of organisation.

The functions of key care staff

Table 5.15 illustrates the differences between the centres in terms of the number and type of staff employed, and the type and size of location. For example, there were six full-time social workers in Leeds, two full-time social workers in Manchester, and none in the Oxford centre. The number of beds in Tower Hamlets and Oxford were similar but the latter employed a much greater number of nursing staff.

It was necessary to examine, therefore, whether these differences in staffing policy were also reflected in the functions that staff carried out and the goals they sought to achieve in so doing.

Information was collected from the staff by means of interviews and self-completion questionnaires. Staff were asked for their perception of goals of the centre (or hospital ward), about their role, their likes and dislikes concerning their work and the inherent stresses. They were also asked about the part they played in the decision-making structure, their roles and functions and the provision of support and supervision.

Directors/Co-ordinators

All the directors and co-ordinators had as their goals the assessment, medical care, social work support and referral of problem drinkers.

The directors and consultant psychiatrists shared very similar roles, functions and responsibilities. They had overall responsibility for clinical work, planning and development of their ward, the management of patients and training.

The officer in charge at Tower Hamlets was responsible for the administration, staffing, financial management, nursing care and pastoral counselling. Her equivalent at Leeds, the centre co-ordinator, was responsible for the overall day-to-day management of the centre. He was responsible for staff supervision, training and development and was expected to meet and co-ordinate nursing, social work and home care staff. He was also concerned with public relations and with facilitating co-ordination and liaison with outside agencies.

Doctors

All the doctors whether registrars, senior registrars, GPs or clinical assistants shared the common goals of ensuring the effective assessment, treatment of patients and support of other staff. At Oxford, Manchester and Portsmouth they were responsible additionally for ensuring that counselling was provided and discharge arrangements were made.

Nurses

The nurses at the various centres also shared common goals: those of providing medical care and social work support. They aimed to maintain a high standard of nursing and in doing this assist patients to return to the community and to cope more effectively within it. The nurses were conscious of their role to support, train and supervise other nursing grades.

The nurses shared the functions of assessment, observation, giving out of medication, running groups, counselling, administration, ward management and liaison with medical staff. They attended and contributed to case conferences, sorted out informal contacts with patients and gave primary health care.

Care/Nursing assistants

At Leeds, Tower Hamlets and Manchester, care/nursing assistants worked in teams to assist the nurses with many of these tasks. Their goals were to assist the drying out of problem drinkers and to help them to overcome their problems. They shared the common basic nursing tasks of ensuring that patients attended to their personal hygiene and had an adequate diet, and helping with general maintenance such as making beds, cleaning up, etc. They helped with record keeping, giving out medication, and with counselling and observation of patients. They all participated in team meetings and liaised with patients and staff.

The centre at Tower Hamlets was reliant on care assistants to observe, consult and inform trained staff about the conditions of patients and to organise the patients and provide them with support.

Table 5.15 Centre Staff and Management

	Leeds	Manchester	Oxford	Tower Hamlets	Portsmouth
Governing Body	St Ann's Shelter and Housing Action	Department of Psychiatry	Oxford Area Health Authority	Salvation Army	Portsmouth and South-east Hants Health Authority
Directors and/or Co-ordinators	W. Kilgallon, Director, St Anne's J. Wymark-Hoar, (co-ordinator/social worker)	Dr B. Hore (medical director/ consultant psychiatrist)	Dr F. Arroyave (medical director/ consultant psychiatrist	Captain Christine Johnston (officer in charge/nursing sister)	Pink Villa & Nelson Ward – Dr Brunning Solent Ward – Dr Fleming and Dr Bale King Villa – Dr Abramczuk and Dr Renton (consultant psychiatrist)
Number of Staff Doctors	2 GPs on call 24 hours; visit 3 times a week. Consultant psychiatrist visit minimum once a week	Consultant psychiatrist 3 research registrars	Consultant psychiatrist; clinical assistant, 2 full-time registrars (on 6 monthly rota)	2 GPs visit once a week	Each ward has half-time consultant, half-time registrar, 1 duty doctor

Nurses	6 charge nurses providing 24 hour cover	½ nursing officer, 3 charge nurses, 1 staff nurse, 3 SENs providing 24 hour cover	½ nursing officer, 3 charge nurses, 6 staff nurses providing 24 hour cover 1 community psychiatric nurse	1 nursing sister, (+ occasional sessions by hostel nurse) on call 24 hours*	2 charge nurses, 2–3 staff nurses per ward giving 24 hour cover student nurses Each ward had an OT attached to it, except Nelson Ward
Care Assistants/ Auxiliary	5 care assistants	6 nursing assistants		5 care assistants	
Social Workers (+ associated posts)	6 social workers	2 full time social workers	1 OT (occasional) 1 information + research officer (half-time)	1 social worker	Hospital social work department
	Project administrator and secretarial staff	5 clerks, Hospital admin staff	Hospital admin staff	1 secretary, Salvation Army admin staff	Hospital admin staff
Type of Location	Hostel Community	Hospital	Hospital	Hostel/lodging house	Hospital
Size	15 Detox beds 5 After-care beds 4 Holding room beds	6 Stage I treatment cubicles 9 Stage II beds	8 beds	9 beds	General wards: Solent ward – 32 beds King Villa – 36 beds Pink Villa – 22 beds Nelson Ward, ATU – 9 beds for men 3 beds for women

*This level of nursing provision was unusual. A SEN was to be appointed

Care/nursing assistants performed both basic nursing and social functions, albeit to different degrees at different centres. Their work complemented that of social workers and senior nurses; that is except in part at Tower Hamlets where they carried out the tasks more usually done by nurses, presumably because of the limited number of professional staff available.

Social workers

The social workers in the specialist centres shared the dual goals of encouraging good relationships between patients and staff, and motivating patients to help themselves. At Portsmouth the social work department did not have a policy about work with problem drinkers and not all the social workers thought it an appropriate use of their time to help them. Any help that was provided was intended to assist the patient in achieving the goal of sobriety.

The primary functions of the social workers were to assess, counsel, sort out material problems and to do casework for personal and drinking problems.

Occupational therapists

The goal of the occupational therapists at Portsmouth was to help acute admission patients become fit for a normal life in a community. (No information was obtained from the OT at Oxford as no OT sessions were being carried out in the detox at the time.) Their function was to assess patients, to organise a realistic rehabilitation programme for them and to carry it out. They were concerned with socialisation, relaxation, physical fitness, work routine and job finding. This was done by both one-to-one counselling and groups.

Comment

Although the number and types of staff employed varied across centres, the staff's description of their roles, goals and nature of work was very similar.

The differences found were of degree: the nurses at Oxford, for example, performed many more of the tasks associated with social work than did their counterparts in Leeds and Portsmouth. The role of the nurses at Oxford no doubt had much to do with the absence of social work staff; however, it also evolved from a belief that nurses had a major part to play in the emotional development of problem drinkers.

The range of tasks and responsibilities of the care/nursing assistants appeared to be related to the number of professional staff also employed. At Leeds the nurses and care assistants worked in teams, the care assistants complementing the particular skills of the nurses; at Tower Hamlets there were many more care assistants than nurses and they therefore performed a number of key nursing functions.

Accountability, support and supervision

The rationale for the staffing policies and practices adopted can only be appreciated when viewed in the light of each centre's particular resources, philosophy and relationship to the parent organisation. Furthermore, the quality of the work of the staff and their achievements can be properly assessed only if the nature of their working environments is taken into account. The provision of support and supervision is of particular importance; this type of work is very demanding of staff because of the high turnover of clientele and could result in low job satisfaction and low morale. Preliminary studies in Leeds showed this to be the case.

Directors/Co-ordinators
Although the directors/consultant psychiatrists retained responsibility for clinical matters, they all delegated day-to-day care of patients to ward teams. These teams were, to different degrees, run on democratic/multidisciplinary lines. Manchester and Oxford were the most explicitly democratic in their approach. Nelson Ward was organised on a similar basis; more so than at Pink Villa, a difference that was deliberate on the part of the consultant psychiatrist responsible for them. The assumption was that a short-term admission ward required one form of ward organisation and a long-term another.

The consultants expected to be consulted about any policy changes, financial and clinical matters to do with the hospital and to be informed about any problems on the wards, external relationships and patients' progress, both in hospital and during follow-up.

The officer in charge at Tower Hamlets had overall responsibility for the work of the centre and if she had specific problems she could refer them to her superiors within the Salvation Army. Any decisions she made could be rescinded by these superiors; in practice this was unlikely but it was expected she would consult them before decisions were made concerning residents, the general running and up-keep of the centre and financial matters. In addition, she met with an advisory group bi-annually and attended a quarterly co-ordinating meeting for those running alcohol services. She was to be informed of decisions made by staff in her absence, of the running of the rest of the hostel complex and decisions made by other nurses. She encouraged all staff to participate in the daily staff meeting which she regularly attended.

The Leeds centre was akin to the one in Oxford in having an explicit democratic/multidisciplinary style of management. The centre had weekly staff meetings, bi-weekly meetings with the staff on the project and a weekly supportive unstructured group. The centre co-ordinator described himself as being 'the centre of a caring team'; his role was to facilitate team decision making and to ensure that the decisions made were acted upon. He was accountable to the project director who in turn was answerable to the council of management.

Doctors
The hospital doctors were supervised by their consultant and saw themselves as members of multidisciplinary teams, unlike the general practitioners who attended sessionally. None of the GPs attended the centre meetings nor did they see themselves as being supervised. The registrars at Oxford described themselves as being supervised by the ward team, the clinical assistant and consultant psychiatrist. The clinical assistant was responsible for the medical practice, administration and supervision. At Manchester the doctors were accountable to the consultant. Their research was supervised by the Professor of Psychiatry.

All the doctors expected to be consulted about clinical decisions and informed about any changes in ward or centre policy. Members of teams also expected to be consulted about non-medical matters, especially if these concerned admissions, discharge, transfer and clearance from first stage beds.

Nurses
All the nurses were members of multidisciplinary teams but the extent to which they were accountable elsewhere reflected the hierarchy specific to their institution. At Leeds they were answerable to the centre co-ordinator; at Tower Hamlets to the officer in charge; at Oxford and Manchester to the nursing officer and the consultant psychiatrist. In Portsmouth the nurses were part of a large management structure including nursing officers and senior and divisional nursing officers.

The various nursing officers attached to the centres shared responsibility for routine administration, staff development, training, and development of new projects and the monitoring of them. The nursing officer at Oxford was also responsible for maintaining the fabric of the building and for liaising with domestic staff. Occasionally he provided social skills training, helped in the hostel associated with the centre and supervised out-patient appointments.

All the nurses expected to be consulted about specific arrangements for patients and to be informed of any changes that were to be implemented in ward policy. Few of the nurses regarded themselves as having much formal supervision, other than in Portsmouth. Instead they saw themselves as consulting other team members or senior staff when required. At Oxford, however, it was stressed that informal supervision was built into case conferences and assessment.

Care/Nursing assistants

Senior nursing staff and ward teams supervised care/nursing assistants at the three hospitals. At Portsmouth supervision was particularly important as it was part of the student/pupil nurse training. However, in Leeds care assistants participated in the democratic structure and were answerable to the centre co-ordinator and in Tower Hamlets they were answerable to the officer in charge.

The care/nursing assistants tended to regard themselves as informally rather than formally supervised other than in Portsmouth. At Tower Hamlets the onus was on the care assistants to consult other staff and to seek advice when required. Those assistants who were part of the democratic teams expected to be consulted about admissions, treatment plans and discharges and informed about any changes that affected their work, whereas at the other centres they did not expected to be so fully involved.

Social workers

The structures for accountability for this staff group were similar to those for nurses. The hospital social workers were members of ward teams and part of a line management structure and were therefore accountable to their seniors and to the appropriate social work departments. At Tower Hamlets the social worker was answerable to the officer in charge; at Leeds the social workers were answerable to their team and the centre co-ordinator.

At Portsmouth the social workers had one-to-one supervision with their senior while those at Manchester, Leeds and Tower Hamlets reported having little formal supervision and instead sought advice and consultation from senior medical and social work staff.

The social workers were akin to the nurses in expecting to be consulted about arrangements concerning patients and informed about any changes in policy that affected them, both directly and indirectly.

Occupational therapists

The occupational therapists at Portsmouth had an equivalent structure to that for the nurses. They were accountable to their seniors, heads of department, their ward team and to the consultant psychiatrist. They expected to be consulted about matters to do with patients and informed about changes in hospital and ward policy.

Comment

The structures within which the various staff groups work appeared broadly to reflect the kind of institution housing the detox centre rather than something inherent to the work itself. However, the emphasis on democratic/multidisciplinary teams at Oxford and

Manchester and the extent to which this was shared in the different setting in Leeds indicated the existence of common assumptions concerning the most appropriate style of staff organisation for the effective management of detoxification – whether it be in a hospital or community-based setting.

Staff morale and job satisfaction

The following descriptions were elicited by means of a content analysis of interviews with staff. All staff in specialist centres enjoyed their work because it provided variety, stimulus, a challenge and allowed them to fulfil a desire to help people. They derived satisfaction from working with problem drinkers per se. Not surprisingly, all of them felt particularly positive about their role, especially when successful in helping someone. At Portsmouth these views were shared by the staff at Nelson Ward and by some doctors and nurses in the general wards.

Much that influenced job satisfaction was located in the structure and ethos of centres or was associated with the characteristics of their client groups. Staff that were part of multidisciplinary teams, and especially those that were run democratically, were very positive about the freedom this gave them to use their initiative and to influence the nature of their work. Nurses particularly enjoyed having more authority than they would have in more traditionally run wards. At Leeds they particularly liked the casual atmosphere that was for them so very different from more formal work in hospitals.

However, some doctors, although committed to the notion of multidisciplinary teams, found it difficult to adjust to their egalitarian nature. This style of work also involved greater responsibility for staff and required them to do a wider range of tasks than was normal on wards. This was particularly the case for care assistants and to a lesser extent for nurses. Also, special difficulties were apparent if relationships within these teams broke down and time and emotional energy was taken up in dealing with, or not dealing with, the issues that were brought to light.

Although staff in specialist centres were interested in problem drinkers and had chosen to work with them, they recognised a number of stresses inherent in doing so. Many of them were frustrated with having to turn people away and in seeing them leave early in ill health, only to return to poor conditions. In particular, the nurses and care assistants, and especially at Leeds and Manchester, saw readmissions as a sign of failure. Patients who were manipulative or who were thought to be potentially aggressive or violent were particularly stressful; although the latter occurred infrequently. At Leeds the staff were conscious of the difficulty of maintaining long-term goals given the high turnover of residents and were saddened to see some of them deteriorate over time.

The staff at Tower Hamlets, Leeds and Oxford expressed frustration at their inability to help people sufficiently due to lack of resources, especially of after care. Similarly, at Oxford they felt limited by the amount of crisis intervention they could provide since they had no means to extend it. At Leeds the nurses felt constrained from taking holidays, or being away ill, because the number of staff employed did not allow for it if the centre was to be adequately manned 24 hours a day, seven days a week. The nurses felt overloaded particularly at weekends when only they and the care assistants were on duty. The lack of staff, too, tied them to the centre and their duty rota prevented them from fully participating in the democratic structure. These constraints also affected the care assistants.

Staff at Portsmouth were much more ambivalent about the satisfaction of working with problem drinkers and some were not as inclined to attribute difficulties to the lack of resources, etc. Their attitudes appeared to fall into three categories: nurses and doctors whose attitudes were similar to those of specialist centre staff; those doctors and nurses who regarded problem drinkers as appropriate patients, who were challenging to work with but who at the same time posed special management problems when mixed with the other psychiatric groups; and nurses and social workers who felt disinclined to work with this group. They saw drinkers' problems as self inflicted and regarded them as difficult, demanding and manipulative people.

It appears from the interviews that there may have been a relationship between the negative view of nurses and the context in which they experienced working with problem drinkers. Many of them found the repeated admissions of problem drinkers frustrating as they felt they could do nothing to change this pattern of behaviour. To their mind, drinkers were being dried out and sent out, only to return again for drying out. In doing so, they used up valuable beds and created difficulties in the management of wards and in the running of ward groups.

Other more diverse factors affected staff job satisfaction. At Oxford, Tower Hamlets and some of the general wards at Portsmouth, staff had considerable work-loads, especially of administrative tasks, which were further aggravated by constant telephone calls, etc. This was particularly so for the nurses, the research and information officer at Oxford and for the officer in charge and care assistants at Tower Hamlets. The care assistants also felt isolated on occasions and were aware of the weight of responsibility they had for dealing with a wide range of problems. At Leeds they felt the strain of having an ill-defined role, which some thought did not give them enough responsibility and opportunities for using their initiative.

Less than adequate working conditions further compounded the difficulties faced by staff at some centres. There was very restricted office space at Oxford and only limited room at Manchester in which staff could meet. At some centres a number of nurses and nursing/care assistants felt unhappy about the poor relations between them and their hierarchy.

Staff length of stay

Two useful measures of the impact of the factors affecting job satisfaction are the rate of turnover of staff and their length of stay.

The highest rate of turnover was amongst care and nursing assistants; otherwise there appeared to have been no significant difference between staff groups. Of those still in post, the shortest lengths of stay were amongst the nurses and social workers at Leeds and the social workers at Manchester. Of those who had left, the shortest lengths of stay were for the administrative and clerical workers at Manchester, the nursing sisters, assistant nurses and care assistants at Tower Hamlets.

The range of lengths of stay suggests that at each centre staff either came and stayed for some time or left relatively quickly. Staff either liked working at a centre and stayed or did not and left. Apparently, it was fairly common for centres to have a core of established staff working alongside others who were much less experienced and who may or may not have stayed for very long. Whether or not this situation was a problem must have depended on the rate at which staff came and went and to what extent.

The attitudes and therapeutic commitment of staff to problem drinkers

The Alcohol and Alcohol Problems Perception Questionnaire (AAPPQ) was used as a means of examining staff experience and attitudes towards working with drinkers at Portsmouth, Oxford and Tower Hamlets. Where possible, compatible information was collated from centre documents for Leeds and Manchester as this sub-study was initiated after work had finished at the designated centres. AAPPQ is made up of a number of scales, including a summary scale, which are concerned with motivation to work with drinkers, expectations of satisfaction, sense of self-esteem in the role, sense of role adequacy and of role legitimacy. It has been demonstrated that these scales are strongly related to the amount of experience people have had working with drinkers, the amount of support they can expect in their role and personality factors such as self-esteem (Cartwright, A., 1980). It has been found that role support and experience are the factors most amenable to the nature of a working environment and are most commonly found in agencies or institutions that specialise in work with drinkers. It is the presence of these factors which very largely explains the difference in overall therapeutic attitudes or commitment between specialist and non-specialist agencies.

The experience of centre staff in working with problem drinkers

Leeds
The nurses were all experienced in psychiatric nursing. The care assistants had more diverse backgrounds; many had been chosen because they had been problem drinkers themselves, and also in some cases had been vagrant, experiences which were considered invaluable in supporting men, especially in the holding room. The co-ordinator and the majority of social workers were qualified and/or had worked in projects for homeless/problem drinkers. This also applied to the director. At the beginning of the experimental period all the staff had gone through an intensive training course specially arranged by a national agency for alcohol education.

Manchester
This centre, too, had a number of established and experienced staff: the nursing officer had previously worked in a centre in Scotland, the co-ordinator (social worker) in a well-known rehabilitation hostel for alcoholics in south London and the medical director had long specialised in the treatment of problem drinkers and the development of services for them. The nurses worked both in the ATU and the centre, on rotation. Some of the nursing assistants were recovered alcoholics, and like their counterparts in Leeds, selected with this experience in mind.

Tower Hamlets
All eight staff working at the centre at the time of the study completed the AAPPQ. The officer in charge and the social worker had had considerable experience of helping problem drinkers. The secretary was also very familiar with the problems of this group having worked at the centre for the last six years.

This group of small but experienced staff was assisted by fairly young and much less experienced care assistants. The general practitioner attached to the centre had had no previous experience of working with problem drinkers.

Oxford
Twenty out of 26 staff completed the AAPPQ. This centre, like Tower Hamlets, had a core group of very experienced and established staff and others who were less so. The former group were largely made up of charge and staff nurses plus the consultant

psychiatrist who was a specialist in the treatment of problem drinkers. The remainder of the staff were inexperienced with problem drinkers, either because they were new, or students or registrars on six-monthly rotation. The nursing officer and the research and information worker had worked there for some years and were therefore also very familiar with the problems of those who abused alcohol.

Portsmouth
Questionnaires were sent to all care staff at the hospital. Only a small proportion were returned despite considerable effort on the part of the research team and heads of departments, some of whom went to great lengths to persuade staff to fill them in. In an attempt to clarify the reasons for this poor return, a member of the research team discussed the matter with staff on the wards. It was clear that staff found the questions about their attitudes to, and experience of, working with problem drinkers very threatening and were not assured by the various arrangements made for confidentiality, and anonymity. Noticeably no problems of this kind were encountered at the other centres.

Over half the questionnaires were returned by nurses; however, very few were returned by registrars, nursing officers and occupational therapists and none by the social workers.

The attitudes of centre staff towards working with problem drinkers

The attitudes of staff, that is on their motivation to work with drinkers, expectations of satisfaction, sense of self-esteem in their role, sense of role adequacy and of legitimacy were compared across and within centres. In the latter case responses from staff working in specialist treatment units (either part- or full-time) were separated from those of the staff only working in centres or general wards; it was thought important to explore whether it was a qualitatively different experience for staff if their work was primarily concerned with the short-term activity of managing withdrawal as compared with providing long-term treatment and rehabilitation.

It was found that specialist centres (Oxford, Tower Hamlets and Nelson Ward at Portsmouth) had high levels of experienced staff and high levels of support for them.

There were particularly low levels of experience and support amongst staff in the general psychiatric wards at Portsmouth, especially compared to the very high levels for staff at the ATU. Tower Hamlets also showed high levels of experience and support. Consistent with these findings were the high levels of overall therapeutic attitude found in Nelson Ward and Tower Hamlets and the lowest in the general wards at Portsmouth.

However, it was also the case that the scores for overall therapeutic attitudes were comparatively low for staff working full-time in the centre at Oxford; lower than for the staff who worked both in the ATU or part-time in the centre and ATU. Hence, it is indicated that working full-time in the centre was in some sense different from doing so part-time. The centre staff at Oxford also had the lowest level of support of all the specialist centres in this sub-study, although they were fairly experienced staff. This group was also low on satisfaction which suggests that the fairly low overall therapeutic attitudes of this group mentioned earlier may be attributed to their perception of not having had the level of support they required to fulfil their role.

It was noticeable that the staff showed a low level of role legitimacy in Tower Hamlets; that is, the staffs' perception of their right to ask clients about their drinking, and clarity, or lack of it, about their responsibility for helping clients. High overall therapeutic attitudes might be expected at Tower Hamlets given the experience and support of staff; however, the scores for role legitimacy were much lower than anticipated. This may well be the influence of the group of young inexperienced care assistants who had a considerable amount of responsibility.

Conclusions

The specialist centres had the advantage of having staff who wanted to work with problem drinkers and could therefore maintain positive attitudes towards them despite the difficulties they encountered with clients in the face of frustration created by limited resources.

The adoption of a multidisciplinary approach made working in specialist centres particularly attractive to staff, especially if the centres operated democratically.

Staff who worked in the non-specialist setting at Portsmouth were much more likely to be ambivalent in their attitudes. They may have been inclined to have more negative attitudes towards problem drinkers because of the various management problems they created, given the way in which services were organised.

A characteristic of these centres was a relatively high turnover of people, many of whom had complex and deep-rooted social and psychological problems. In such settings staff had to work to immediate short-term goals and face the arduous task of combining these with more significant long-term goals. The finding at Oxford, that experienced staff working in the centre full-time scored lower on satisfaction and role support as compared to those who worked part-time in the centre and ATU, is consistent with other research findings. Various authors have stressed that it is important to staff job satisfaction that they have opportunities to work with clients on a longer-term basis as well as the short term. Working with a high turnover of people with acute and chronic needs affects staff morale as it allows them few opportunities to observe the results of the time, energy and care they have invested.

These difficulties were further compounded in centres that had little control over the nature and timing of admissions, because of policies that required them to take people when brought by the police, etc. Also, where the target group was single homeless people, who often suffered from many physical as well as emotional and housing problems, this could be more demanding of staff.

A particularly vulnerable group were the care assistants whose need for support and supervision was often very evident. It appeared to be possible for staff to work effectively under these conditions if at least some of the following features prevailed: regular support and supervision, clear tasks and well-defined roles, a decision-making structure that facilitated participation and which maintained a balance between responsibility and authority. Also, it was necessary for a centre to have a core of experienced staff, facilities for staff training and development, adequate present and future funding and sufficient back-up facilities.

The implications of this sub-study seem to be that specialist centres were more likely to have staff whose attitudes were positive, and therefore beneficial, to problem drinkers. This is because staff there felt they had a legitimate role, sufficient support to maintain satisfaction in their work and/or had opportunities to work with drinkers in a variety of settings, especially those providing more long-term treatment and rehabilitation.

LIAISON, CO-OPERATION AND CO-ORDINATION WITH OTHER AGENCIES

Two assumptions can be made about the nature of inter-agency liaison, co-ordination and co-operation: (1) that the non-statutory sector is the primary provider of services for problem drinkers and (2) that the nature and quality of relationships between services is important to the effectiveness of treatment. Two major areas of difficulty may be anticipated: those encountered in attempting to forge close working links between non-statutory and statutory agencies and the detrimental effect of the non-statutory sector's tendency to be fragmented and territorial.

This section is therefore concerned with the operation of the centres' relationships across both statutory and non-statutory agencies.

Table 5.16 Local specialist agencies for problem drinkers and single homeless people over 25 years

		Leeds	Manchester	Oxford	Tower Hamlets	Portsmouth
Non-statutory						
Residential	Rehabilitation hostel	6**	7**	2**	3	–
	Assessment unit	–	–	–	2**	–
	Night shelter	3	3	1	1	5
Day Provision	Day advisory support centre	1**	2	1**	1	–
	Counselling service	1	1	–	1	–
	Day shelter	1**	1	1	3	1
Statutory						
Residential	Reception centre	1	1	–	–	–
	ATU	–*	2**	1**	–	1**
Day Provision	Homeless offenders unit	1	1	1	–	–
	Probation day centre	–	1	1	–	–
Co-ordination	Non-statutory	1	1	1	1	–
	Statutory	–	–	–	–	1

*The Regional ATU was some miles away. However they had close working links with the centre
** Associated with centre parent project

Co-ordination

Detox centres have the common goal of providing care for people, within their target population, when intoxicated and detoxicating. If centres are to do more for their clients, they must be able to offer them opportunities for treatment and rehabilitation either on the premises or by referral elsewhere. The latter is naturally dependent on such services being available locally, or within reasonable distance; however, successful referral requires rather more. The functioning of a system of services is largely determined by the quality of relations between the agencies involved, at both executive and grass-roots levels. Key factors affecting relationships are likely to be the extent to which agencies: recognise their interdependence, in terms of the frequency of meetings and the discussion of common difficulties; collectively plan new developments; and ensure staff have the time to attend meetings, working parties, etc.

Agencies that are part of a larger parent organisation incorporating a range of services must have the advantage of maintaining good co-ordination, as must those in areas that have local co-ordinating agencies.

Table 5.16 shows the specialist agencies for problem drinkers and the single homeless that were located near each of the centres, and whether they were associated with the centres or their parent projects.

The centres at Manchester, Leeds and Oxford were similar in that they were all part of a network of services related in some way to their parent organisation. They also had assistance from a local co-ordinating agency.

The Salvation Army ran another agency in Tower Hamlets. There was a co-ordinating agency in the borough of which staff were active members. At Portsmouth there was very little, apart from the ATU; the statutory co-ordinating service was located in the social services department and made little direct contact with hospital staff.

Interagency meetings for co-operation and liaison

As a means of examining the nature and extent of co-operation and liaison, a content analysis was done of the minutes of the meetings of local agencies which had these functions. Information was extracted on attendance of centre staff, mention made about the centre and the contribution of centre staff. To allow for a fuller picture than the minutes could allow, centre staff were also interviewed about their attitudes and experience.

The co-ordinating agencies from whom minutes were obtained were as follows:

Leeds

Detoxification Advisory Committee (every 2 months)
This committee comprised representatives from Alcoholics Anonymous (AA), DHSS, the social services, police, probation service and various members of the detoxification centre's management and staff.

Community Services Meeting (CSM) (monthly)
Representatives from any agency concerned with the home-based alcoholics and homeless alcoholics were entitled to attend. It was set up and maintained by the St Anne's Project, and in particular by the community social worker from the centre.

Manchester

Multi-Facilities Group (monthly)
This group was set up and was serviced by the Greater Manchester Council on Alcoholism to co-ordinate and develop services for problem drinkers in the area.

Joint Care Planning Team (JCPT) (monthly)
JCPT was part of the area health authority structure and was responsible for the planning and development of joint health and social services. It was made up of officers from health and social service departments and representatives from key local agencies.

Oxford

Berkshire Council on Alcoholism (every six to eight weeks) &
Oxford and District Council on Alcoholism (ODCA) (every two to three months)
These councils on alcoholism were set up to develop a range of education, training and counselling services in their areas. The committees were made up of representatives from statutory, non-statutory agencies and other interested persons.

Tower Hamlets

No Fixed Abode (NFA) (every two months)
NFA was a co-ordinating agency for those working with single homeless people and problem drinkers in Tower Hamlets and adjoining boroughs of east London. Its committee was made up of representatives from agencies, statutory services and other interested persons.

Portsmouth

Portsmouth Council for Community Services (PCCS) (every three months)
PCCS was set up to promote services for a broad range of deprived groups. Its committee meeting was made up of a wide range of

representatives from statutory and non-statutory advice and service agencies.

Hampshire Council on Alcoholism (every three months)
The Council of Alcoholism aimed to promote the development of services; it also provided a counselling service based in Southampton. The committee was made up of representatives from statutory, non-statutory agencies and other interested individuals.

Leeds

Detox Advisory Committee — membership and functioning The representative from AA (who was also the chairman of the meeting), the police liaison officer, the representative from the DHSS Social Work Services Group, and the centre co-ordinator, were the most regular attendants of this meeting. All attended at least four out of five meetings. The representative from social services, the project director and members of the detox centre staff attended three out of the five meetings. Representatives from the probation office and the social worker responsible for the after-care houses came infrequently, attending only one or two meetings out of the five.

As might be expected, the issues discussed in these meetings centred largely around the functions and policies of the detox centre. The committee gave particular consideration to the patterns of admission, length of stay and referral procedures. Special 'work groups' were established by the Advisory Committee to study particular aspects of these issues in greater detail. To facilitate the work of the meetings and the work groups, statistics were often provided by the centre co-ordinator. The second most recurrent area for discussion were police procedures and practices, and negotiations for the project's future developing and long-term funding. The committee also regularly discussed, although less frequently, the record keeping of the project and the importance of research.

Touched on, although less regularly, were issues to do with staffing, building maintenance, the after-care facilities and the details of the medical provision in the centre.

The minutes showed that the Advisory Committee was appropriately named. It provided a forum for discussion, for sounding out ideas and policy changes and for ensuring that the detox centre was aware of other agencies' opinions and expectations of it. The Advisory Committee has been especially useful in encouraging the co-operation of the major statutory bodies, apart from health authorities who have not been represented.

Community Services Meeting — membership and functioning Of ten meetings for which minutes were obtained, five were selected at random to cover a range of meetings in 1977 and 1978.

Over the two years, a wide range of agencies sent representatives to these meetings. They included the Reception Centre, the local council on alcoholism, the probation service, council for voluntary service, Salvation Army, Common Lodging House managers, GPs, St George's Crypt, and of course the staff of the detox centre and of the St Anne's Project Day Shelter. However, their rates of attendance were found to vary considerably. The most regular attenders in both years were the staff of the detox centre and of the Shelter and the probation service.

Each of these attended three or four meetings out of five. Representatives of the Salvation Army, council on alcoholism and Reception Centre attended twice.

Representatives from the St George's Crypt and the council for voluntary service were minuted for the first year but not the second. Two Common Lodging House managers and a GP who worked with the homeless attended only in the second year, although on a fairly regular basis.

The most common topics for discussion in these meetings were problems of co-ordination. These problems occurred both between the agencies attending the meeting, and between them and other agencies such as the DHSS Supplementary Benefit Office. Initiatives for discussing and acting on these issues were spread evenly across the agencies attending. So although the St Anne's Project was mainly responsible for maintaining the meetings, it did not dominate them. There was also regular but less frequent discussion of the strategies and political manoeuvres required to develop specialist services for the single homeless, and particularly medical services for this client group. The remainder of these meetings was spent dealing with immediate crises, such as the rehousing of men from the Grove Hostel after a serious fire there, and in straightforward sharing of information. This would include news of project developments, of accommodation vacancies, and of any developments in solving common problems, such as in obtaining employment for clients.

The minutes of the Community Services Meeting showed that membership did fluctuate and at times there were too few attenders to really merit the time spent. However, when sufficient people attended, the meeting was a useful forum of discussion and co-operation between the agencies concerned.

Within the limits of the two structures for communication detailed above, the detox centre was holding discussions with all the major relevant statutory agencies, with the exception of the two major hospitals within Leeds, St James' and the Leeds General Infirmary. However, the St Anne's Project had close links with one local Community Health Council and the Family Practitioner Committee. The links between the detox centre and statutory agencies were further strengthened by the membership structure of the Board of Management.

Indeed, not only was the centre integrated at executive and/or grass-roots level but was largely instrumental in establishing and maintaining these structures for communication and co-operation.

Tower Hamlets

The other community-based non-statutory agency studied was less extensively involved in comparison with that at Leeds. Two Tower Hamlets' staff were recorded as attending 19 (73 per cent) out of 26 NFA meetings and spoke at eight of them. They spoke about the present state of the centre; that is — its referrals, turnover and staffing. They also helped with negotiations with a local agency that had been causing some concern and actively encouraged representation from other Salvation Army centres in the area. It was evident from the minutes that one staff member was on the NFA finance subcommittee and that she and other staff contributed to various day events and meetings with statutory authorities. The Salvation Army colonel responsible for the centre was also known to attend national meetings concerned with provision for problem drinkers and occasional meetings with funders.

Manchester

The centre staff's involvement was on a par with Leeds as they were well represented on their two local committees and regularly participated. Four centre staff attended the multi-facilities group and one very regularly. Three staff attended the JCPT. Staff attended nine out of ten of both meetings and spoke at all but one of them.

The topics covered by staff at the multi-facilities group ranged from the development of new provision, funding and funding crises. They also assisted by intervening when another project had difficulties. At the JCPT they raised points about the implications of centre policy and future plans, assisted in the organisation and running of training and events and helped to set up staff working parties to look at local resources.

As we mentioned earlier, the centre social workers were responsible not only for the support of ex-patients and potential referrals, but for development and support of community facilities. The work of these social workers and the community psychiatric nurse had much to do with the setting up of supported accommodation for ex-patients, and more generally for informal co-ordination of work with the single homeless and problem drinkers.

The medical staff participated in various hospital, area and regional health meetings and one in particular was well known for his work nationally.

Oxford
The staff of the Ley Clinic also actively attended meetings with local agencies and discussed with them problems of service delivery and development, although to a more limited extent than at Manchester or Leeds. Five different clinic staff attended the ODCA meetings. The most regular attenders were the clinical assistant and the nursing officer. The clinic was represented at 18 (86 per cent) out of 21 meetings and spoke at 13 of them. Their contributions primarily concerned the functioning of the Council's hostels (which provided after-care beds for the clinic), and they assisted in the development of more hostels. On a number of occasions they requested that clinic staff be seconded by the council onto training courses.

One staff member regularly attended the Berkshire Council on Alcoholism meetings. She attended 22 (88 per cent) out of 25 meetings and spoke at half of them. Her contribution covered the development of a training course, the need for centre development in the area, information on the Ley Clinic's funding situation and discussions of papers produced by agencies in the area. She was responsible for organising and running a training course for professional volunteers and was assisted in this by Ley Clinic staff.

That the clinic recognised its role in supporting other services and in development is apparent from the work of their information and research officer. Despite heavy commitments of all staff, she had a function (amongst others) to facilitate local co-ordination and the development of services in the region. Although no mention was made in either set of minutes of the needs of the single homeless, it was known that the clinic staff had a close working relationship with the staff of the Oxford Simon Community and with members of the probation service.

Portsmouth
The staff at Portsmouth were much less involved with local agencies. The social work team leader from the hospital attended two out of eight PCCS meetings. The main topic of discussion at these meetings was development of special projects housing for the mentally handicapped, inadequate or mentally disturbed. The team leader's contribution to these meetings was to encourage this initiative and to suggest that two sub-groups be formed to discuss what they should be and how to promote them. A wide range of organisations had representatives on this committee, many of whom also attended one or two of them. St James Hospital was mentioned once in the minutes.

The consultant psychiatrist for the ATU attended Hampshire Council on Alcoholism meetings; he went to eight (57 per cent) out of 14 and spoke at four of them. The topics most often discussed by him were the obtaining of social services permission and suitable premises for a residential project. Other topics that concerned the committee were: the loss of centre beds, a survey of need for them, the negotiations to provide them and provision of training for volunteers in counselling.

St James Hospital had a community nursing officer, responsible for the work of the community psychiatric nurses and for the management of the hospital's housing association accommodation. The emphasis of his work was the support of ex-patients and rather less on assisting in the co-ordination of services. He recognised the necessity for the latter but felt unable to carry out both functions well, in the time available. It was hoped that the proposed community psychiatric nurse (to specialise in problem drinkers) might take on a liaison/co-ordination role locally.

Liaison with statutory services

As was mentioned earlier, an effective partnership between statutory and non-statutory agencies is essential to the provision of comprehensive services in an area. However, it is not uncommon for there to have been problems in the development of this partnership, if indeed one had been established. In order to explore these issues, information was collected during the pilot phase at Leeds on liaison between the two major statutory agencies, the social work and probation services, and the centre.

Parallel information was not collected elsewhere because of other research priorities. However limited this information may be, it was thought of value to present the Leeds experience, as a number of points were found, informally, to be relevant for other centres.

Local authority social services department
In general there was relatively little working contact between the local authority social services department and the centre. This was only to be expected since it was known that the type of man likely to be a client of a centre for homeless drunkenness offenders would probably have had very rare contact with local authority social services departments. This was confirmed in a search for any contact between a sample of 20 detox clients with social services departments in Leeds. Only four of these men had had any contact with the department in the previous four years, and all four were contacts on a single occasion. Two were for minor pieces of advice, whilst the other two were examples of the only contact of any recurrence between the local department and the centre – namely the centre referring men to the local authority in the hope of obtaining specialist residential accommodation for them. For various reasons, these requests were largely unsuccessful. In the cases of the two in the sample, one was referred for consideration for a place in a hostel for

the mentally ill, but the client refused the place offered, whilst the other referral was for consideration for Part III accommodation. The application was turned down because psychiatric reports mentioned that the man was incontinent, and that he was a chronic alcoholic, which was felt to be difficult because of the freedom allowed the residents in aged persons' homes.

Liaison with the probation services
Although there seemed to be little overlap between the work of social workers in the centre and in the local authority, there was a considerable overlap in the cases dealt with by the centre social workers and the probation service, particularly for the homeless offenders unit. This unit had a specialist function of assisting those of no fixed abode, especially if they had been recently discharged from some form of institution. The unit comprised a senior probation officer, six probation officers and three ancillaries, and operated in a similar fashion to a social services intake team. A full-time duty officer interviewed persons of no fixed abode in Leeds who were in some way associated with the police or the courts. This could involve something like two and a half thousand interviews a year, three-fifths of which were with individuals who were never seen again. The senior probation officer for the homeless offenders unit described regular users of his unit as local homeless men or women. About a quarter of the reasons for contact were dealings with the DHSS over finances. Each officer had an on-going caseload of approximately 40 men.

There was no doubt that the unit and the centre had dealt with many of the same people. Many of the centre clients seemed well known to the probation officers. In a pilot study of 20 men, it was found that 15 out of the 20 were known to the homeless offenders unit, including every person in the sample who had made at least five visits to the centre in a two-year career, so repeaters at the centre were all known to the probation service as well.

Probation officers visited their clients whilst they were in the centre and probation officers were sometimes notified by centre social workers of a man's possible whereabouts on his discharge from the centre. However, there was not a great deal of on-going liaison between the centre social workers and the probation officers over particular casework, although there were odd occasions when, for example, probation officers attended the staff meeting at the centre and liaised about accommodation arrangements.

Summary

The staff of designated centres were the most actively engaged in co-operation and liaison. This was apparent in the responsibility they took for promoting the need for a broad range of services; not only for those directly related to their centre, nor necessarily in their catchment area.

These centres were able to do so for a number of pertinent reasons: their operational policies anticipated the need for staff to do development work, members of their parent organisation were also concerned with co-ordination and liaison, and it was recognised as a priority that staff support their local co-ordinating agency and participate in its activities, whether directly related to the centre or not.

The other specialist centres were conscious of the need to liaise and to promote the co-ordination and development of services locally, and therefore supported their local co-ordinating agency. However, they would have extended their activities had they had more staff resources.

The Portsmouth staff attached less importance to links with alcohol and single homeless agencies. The focus there was on services for the mentally ill, etc., within which the needs of the problem drinker were but one of a number of priorities. That liaison was limited might be anticipated as their procedures for referral from general wards was to the ATU or out-patients. Also, the ATU and social work department did not regard it as their responsibility to make after-care arrangements beyond fixing out-patient appointments. Nor did the hospital have special staff available to them to set up and maintain the necessary links.

In Leeds, liaison with statutory services tended to reflect the extent to which the client groups overlapped. The probation service liaised with the centre occasionally over cases and at executive level, the social services less so.

Noticeably effective means of maintaining close working links between statutory and non-statutory services, and across the non-statutory sector, were the advisory committee meetings and those of local co-ordinating agencies. They provided opportunities for regular discussions of policy and practice and for tackling common problems.

It can be concluded that effective co-ordination, liaison and co-operation are vital to the achievement of the system's goals of rehabilitation and treatment of problem drinkers to which centres contribute. If a centre is to be able to play its part within the network of service in its area, sufficient resources are required for it to do so on a consistent basis; this is particularly important where the development of essential services depends on the initiative of centre staff.

6
Discussion and Recommendations

Detoxification, or more precisely, the management of intoxication and withdrawal, occurs in a variety of settings and circumstances. The range of places where this service is provided is illustrated below:
1   beds in general hospitals, usually scattered throughout different wards;
2   beds in general psychiatric hospitals: either together or throughout different wards;
3   at home, supervised by a GP (general practitioner);
4   in hospital accident and emergency departments;
5   in non-statutory agencies, based in the community, run by nurses and supervised by a GP/VMO (Visiting Medical Officer) who is brought in on a sessional basis. Usually such agencies also provide facilities for more long-term rehabilitation;
6   in special units in psychiatric hospitals, usually associated with an alcoholism treatment unit or equivalent;
7   in the sick bay of a DHSS Resettlement Unit for the single homeless, supervised by a VMO.
   The focus of research and service development has been on types (5) and (6) though there has been a recent upsurge of interest in types (1) and (2); the interest in the latter would appear to be due to the limited resources available because of expenditure cuts.

ARE THERE COMMON ELEMENTS IN DETOXIFICATION SERVICES?

Visits to any number of services would soon highlight the difficulties inherent in drawing together the essential features of a detox service, thereby posing problems for any policy makers wishing to establish guidelines for development. One of the distinctive features of this area of provision is the great variety amongst services: no two are the same. What exists varies in terms of:
1   their nature – for example whether drugs are used for withdrawal; if so what and how much; whether social workers are employed; patterns of referral and lengths of stay;

145

2   the target population – whether provision is made for women; for habitual drunken offenders exclusively; and the extent to which clients must be considered sufficiently motivated to deal with their chronic alcohol problems;

3   the use of terms to describe the emotional and physical problems that are being dealt with and the help offered. The term 'detoxification' is sometimes used to describe the physical and psychological effects of withdrawal from alcohol, and sometimes to describe the form of treatment applied to a person and their condition;

4   goals – those most commonly referred to include: management of withdrawal from alcohol; treatment for acute physical or psychological problems; care for chronic physical or psychological difficulties; diversion of habitual drunkenness offenders from the penal system; resettlement of the homeless; and the rationalisation of the use of health and social services by people with drinking problems.

The task of drawing up the common elements of detox services and relating them to resources and outcome is therefore problematic.

That detoxification is so enigmatic can be attributed to its stage in development, not any lack of good sense on the part of policy makers or providers. What is indicated is the need for continuing experiment and research.

WHAT ARE THE EXPECTATIONS FOR DETOXIFICATION SERVICES?

An earlier paragraph indicated the variety of health sectors that are in some way implicated in the functioning of a detox service. The outcome expected or desired by each vary and may even appear contradictory. For example, policy makers in the health services are likely to put particular emphasis on a detox service's impact on health services while police would stress the effect on their procedures and the use of police time. The staff of a detox centre might emphasise the importance of helping clients live a longer and happier life whether or not the centre was economically viable.

The main interest groups and the policy issues associated with them are outlined below:

Penal system

The emphasis for penal policy makers would be the extent to which a detox service could divert the habitual drunkenness offender either at the point of arrest or in court: whether offenders were removed completely or partially from the system and whether there was a subsequent decline in the number of drunkenness offences in an area and in the number imprisoned for non-payment of fines for drunkenness.

Health and social services
One of the key functions of a detox centre is the provision of access to other medical and social services. Since a detox centre is, or should be, part of an overall service, it should be possible to match individual needs to appropriate facilities and to provide the necessary liaison and follow-up. By this means the presence of a detox centre should contribute to the more effective use, by its target population, of specialist and non-specialist services in their area.

Detox centre
A key role of a detox centre is often to confront and influence people who have problems with drinking or drunkenness, and to motivate them to change their behaviour. This means to provide, where appropriate, opportunities for rehabilitation (using the term broadly to include all those facilities essential to improve the emotional and physical well-being of a detox centre user). Opportunities for rehabilitation may occur in the detox centre and/or through the provision of access to other services. At the very least, a detox centre should provide care for its target population when they are intoxicated and withdrawing, which would entail the treatment of immediate psychological and physical conditions: for example, confusion, anxiety and disorientation, and any other condition or ailment that is evident and in need of attention.

Staff
The desire for this group is to help clients in the best way possible and for as long as is required, while retaining a reasonable level of job satisfaction, sense of competence and commitment to the particular regime.

Local community
The experience of community workers in inner city areas is that local people do not like to see individuals or small groups drinking and/or being drunk in local parks and highways or on buses, etc. It is also desired that should anyone require detoxification, services should be readily available to them and sympathetic to their needs.

There is a wide range of interests and expectations involved. However, not all detox services and centres could or should fulfil the range described above. A centre should fulfil the basic function of managing intoxication and withdrawal; any other assessment criteria will depend on each centre's particular goals, target population and on the part they play in the broader system of services, and the goals of that system of services.

ARE DETOXIFICATION CENTRES NECESSARY?

Since the study was mainly concerned with what was being done at the existing centres, how, by whom, and with what results, it was not possible to conclude, per se, whether detoxification centres *should* be set up.

As a means of diverting drunkenness offenders from the penal system, the results of the experimental centres must be seen as, at best, equivocal. Setting up detoxification services introduced new variables and complications which made it difficult to trace any success in responding to public drunkenness. In Leeds, where the effects were examined in most depth, the detoxification system came to operate in addition to the penal system rather than instead of it. Whilst it showed that a facility for habitual drunkenness offenders there would invariably be full, the system required such clients to go through the humiliation of arrest before the provision of help was allowed. The staff had virtually no control over who, when, or how many times clients entered, which proved detrimental to staff morale and resilience, and meant there could never be any planning of overall or individual responses. Since the system was also ineffective in removing offenders from the courts, it must be concluded that the services were obviously meeting widespread needs but were not being provided in an effective manner.

But the failure of detoxification centres to divert habitual drunkenness offenders should not lead to an abandonment of other possible means of responding to the problems of this group. They continue to be a massive waste of police and court resources. The current research has confirmed more strongly than ever that habitual drunkenness offending is a symptom of severe underlying drink problems, and ultimately responding to their drinking will be the most effective way of confronting the problem of offending. For nearly two decades there has been a preoccupation with one particular type of detoxification centre as the only means of responding to this group. In practice, this model has not reduced drunkenness offences. Perhaps their entry point should be different – say after a court hearing or during a period of probation if motivation has been fostered. Perhaps such facilities should not be residential, but function as occasional or day-care services. Alternatively, it might be that other types of response altogether should be tried. Neither should planners of services assume that because detoxification centres did not happen to reduce public drunkenness in Leeds, there is no need for such centres for other client groups. The preoccupation with public inebriates as the supposed 'only' group requiring detoxification has blinded health and social services to the needs of many other problem drinkers who from time to time require care and supervision while they withdraw from alcohol, but who may never have committed any drunkenness offence.

It was clear that there is a need for statutory provision of detoxification; whether it takes the form of the experimental or other centres or something completely new is still debatable.

The study in Portsmouth was an example of an area with no specialist detoxification service. Assuming this area is not atypical, it can be said that detoxification was not as easily accessible as in the areas with specialist facilities. It was also regarded as inappropriate to have to deal with drying out clients in the general admission wards of a psychiatric hospital. The study of the general psychiatric hospital in Portsmouth showed that there were a number of people being referred for the purpose of detoxification; they did not receive the range of help that was made accessible to them at the specialist centres. They were, in fact, perhaps using scarce resources that could have been more appropriately used for people with other problems.

The four specialist centres studied were found to be well utilised by clients who appeared to have a number of alcohol-related problems. In fact, the very existence of the non-experimental specialist centres goes a long way in indicating the demand for services for the management of detoxification. The clientele manifested a range of problems – social, psychological, and physical – and as such the service should be viewed within the framework of a psycho-social model of drinking and drinking problems rather than an exclusively medical approach. Any discussions or assessment of the role of detoxification centres must therefore take account of economic and political factors that determine prevailing attitudes to drinking and drunkenness, and how they shape attempts to deal with the problems they create.

Costs versus benefits?

The cost of setting up a service versus the benefits accrued from it should also be considered. While this was outside the brief of the research team certain recommendations/observations can be made. It was quite clear that the relationship between costs and benefits were not directly correlated. There is a point at which the increased costs do not significantly increase the benefits for the client. The study of the experimental centres showed that detoxification could be managed effectively in a community-based project and that a high complement of medical staff and sophisticated technology was not required. The need for specialist help was small: few people had severe withdrawal symptoms. Thus an expensive, custom-built centre is not necessary. The community-based centre in Leeds was adequate for dealing with this client group. Nevertheless, to be effective, a centre *must* have skilled and committed staff and *must* be an integral part of a range of services, if it is to achieve the goals of diversion and/or rehabilitation. Centres cannot function if their staff are overloaded since they must provide a service to clients, develop services to which clients can be referred and maintain links with these services once they are established. Therefore resources need to be made available for staff for the developmental and follow-up aspects of detox work.

Who formed the client group?

In addressing the question of whether or not detoxification centres are necessary, it is important to consider the level of problem drinking manifested by clients brought into the centres. It was quite evident that habitual drunkenness offenders did not necessarily have a monopoly of either drink-related problems or detoxification attendances as was initially envisaged by the Weiler Report. It clearly was the case that clients who could be found as being habitual drunkenness offenders were much more likely to have a more severe dependence problem than clients who had only been arrested for a drunkenness offence perhaps once or twice in their life. Habitual drunkenness offenders, however, were not the only problem group as could be seen in the Oxford centre where most of the clients had no record of drunkenness offences. These people were clearly suffering from more acute withdrawal symptoms. This group of clients manifested more acute problems compared to the more chronic problems of the clients in the Leeds and Tower Hamlets centres.

It was found that there were three categories who could be considered as being possible clients for detoxification centres. There were:
- occasional drunkenness offenders;
- habitual drunkenness offenders;
- other problem drinkers who were not drunkenness offenders.

Studies of the court records in Leeds demonstrated that the majority of drunkenness offences were committed by persons who were only arrested for this offence in Leeds on one occasion. It was therefore most probable that occasional or one-off drunkenness offenders constitute the bulk of such offenders nationally. In the client characteristic study, persons in detoxification centres who had committed one or two drunkenness offences reporter higher scores on the severity of alcohol dependence questionnaire than non-offenders. Although this cannot provide firm evidence that occasional drunkenness offenders in general are likely to be problem drinkers, it is a possibility which might be looked at in future research. Given the vast numbers involved, it is unrealistic to propose anything other than that for a first offence of drunkenness, offenders should be cautioned or if necessary prosecuted under existing arrangements. Within the three-year study reported, most offenders only appeared once, and it would therefore seem pointless designing a complex and expensive socio-medical response to them all.

Habitual drunkenness offenders can be defined as persons with three or more cautions or charges for drunkenness convictions and are likely to have a significant drinking problem. In the past, 'habitual' offenders have been defined as those who committed three such offences within a 12-month period (Weiler Report, 1971); however, clients who had committed three or more offences at any time showed considerably higher scores than others on the severity of alcohol dependence questionnaire. The questionnaire also indicated other characteristics that will be expected of persons with a chronic drink problem. It may be that once a person has committed more than one drunkenness offence that this is a strong indicator of a possible drink problem. More detailed research will be needed to verify this. However, taking the current evidence in collaboration with that compiled in the Weiler Report, it seems quite clear that persons who have committed more than two drunkenness offences are very likely to have a severe drink problem. They should therefore be the responsibility of the DHSS *and* the Home Office.

More than half the clients referred to the centre at Oxford had never been convicted for drunkenness offences and only a quarter had made three or more offences. Yet almost three-quarters of them were found to have a very serious drinking problem. Thus there is a third group of problem drinkers in need of help and these are also the responsibility of the DHSS.

On average, clients at the two designated centres and at the centre in east London scored higher in terms of alcohol problems than those admitted to Oxford or persons screened out in the admission wards at Portsmouth. Yet the higher incidence of withdrawal symptoms and the heaviest use of drugs in detoxification treatment was at Oxford. It appears that although the overall chronic severity of drinking problems was highest where habitual drunkenness offenders were the majority of clientele, the level of acute problems was highest where they were primarily home-based.

What service should be provided?

It is clear there is not a prototype for a detoxification centre; the most striking features about the five services studied is their lack of uniformity.

However it is possible to relate key centre functions, how they are used and by whom. Factors influencing the type of service are:
- accessibility for potential clients;
- treatment programme – diversity of provision for practical support, emotional help, treatment and rehabilitation;

- continuity of provision within a system of services and referral out;
- specialism.

There are different types of centres that cater for different types of clients; the underlying similarity between clients is that they are all likely to have a drink problem. The ease of accessibility for the different groups will, to some extent, influence the service provided/required.

The centres studied were not only very varied in their mode of operation but also in the people who were admitted to them. They each had different selection criteria and procedures, those admitted were not always within their target population and centres put varying degrees of emphasis on the immediate condition of an individual at admission. The factors to be considered when defining the appropriateness of a group for admission to a centre are:

- extent of withdrawal
- extent of alcohol problem
- extent of immediate needs other than for withdrawal
- extent of long-term problems/disabilities

Being homeless or regularly using cheap single person accommodation is often associated with a range of chronic physical, psychological and financial difficulties. There are particular problems inherent in the way of life of itinerant single homeless people. People with some form of permanent housing are more able to retain contact with a network of family and friends and to make use of the system for health care and personal social services; they are therefore more likely to have a permanent base to which they can return.

Thus the requirements of the different client groups vary according to whether they have acute or chronic drinking problems, social and physical disabilities. The designated centres, by definition, were more likely to admit clients with more chronic problems. This was also true of the Tower Hamlets Centre, while the other specialist centre in Oxford was more likely to admit persons with acute drinking problems although few of these had many social or physical problems. This could in part be due to the accessibility of this service since it required clients to be referred by a general practitioner and to make their own way to the centre which was located on the outskirts of Oxford. Therefore, for a designated centre to be effective it should be located within or very close to the area where most habitual drunkenness offences occur.

What staffing and staff management are required?

To be effective in the long term a centre needs to combine a number of features. A core of staff members who are experienced, skilled and interested in working with problem drinkers thereby ensures positive attitudes to them and familiarity with the types of services available on referral.

It was the norm for staff in centres to be members of a multi-disciplinary team. This type of structure was thought appropriate, given the social, psychological and physical aspects inherent in problem drinking.

The common elements of structure and management in the centres suggest that it was possible for staff to work effectively under quite demanding conditions if at least some of the following features prevailed: regular support and supervision, clear tasks and well defined roles, a decision-making structure that facilitated participation and maintained the balance between responsibility and authority, a core of experienced staff, facilities for staff training and development, adequate present and future funding and, once again, sufficient back-up facilities.

It is evident that staff training, experience, support and supervision are crucial to the effective functioning of a detox centre. Also there are issues specific to working in detox centres and services, not yet incorporated into training courses for people working with problem drinkers (for example the role of care assistants and counselling with short-stay clients). It would therefore be valuable if the DHSS could provide information on what topics might be usefully covered by training courses and advice on which specialists might be brought in to teach them. The DHSS, too, could take the initiative to stimulate appropriate courses by providing the funds for them.

IN CONCLUSION

It is clear that there is a need for services for people who are suffering physical, social and emotional consequences of heavy drinking (either as a manifestation of an acute or chronic problem).

The centres studied have gone a long way towards pinpointing the critical issues and have provided a framework for further experimentation on similar or alternative lines. They have shown quite how extensive these problems are and how important it is for there to be rapid developments in similar and complementary services.

Appendix 1

DRUNKENNESS LAWS

In this report, the term 'drunkenness offence' applies to two types of offence:

(1)   Simple drunkenness, that is, the offence of being found drunk in any highway or other public place whether a building or not, or on any licensed premises (Licensing Act, 1872, s. 12); the expression 'public place' includes any place to which the public have access (Licensing Act 1902, s. 8).

The offence of simple drunkenness is often called 'drunk and incapable'. The term drunk and incapable, for example, was used by the Leeds police and the Leeds court, rather than the term 'simple drunkenness'.

(2)   Drunkenness with aggravation, that is, all offences except simple drunkensss listed in the First Schedule to the Inebriates Act 1898; offences against s. 2 of the Licensing Act 1902; and offences against s. 174 (2) of the Licensing Act 1964.

The offences of drunkenness with aggravation may be of various types, but by far the most common is the offence usually referred to as 'drunk and disorderly'.

A number of changes were made to the punishments for these offences in 1977 and 1978.

Fines

The Criminal Law Act of 1977 (parts of s. 31) which came into force on 8 September 1977 and 17 July 1978, raised the maximum fine for some offences of drunkenness with aggravation and simple drunkenness from £5 to £25, and for others from £10 to £50. The Criminal Justice Act 1967 (commencement No. 4 order 1977), brought into force on 1 February 1978, increased the maximum fines for the offence of drunk and disorderly from £10 to £50.

Imprisonment

The commencement No. 4 order 1977 also abolished imprisonment for the offence of drunk and disorderly. Imprisonment for non-payment of fines had been governed by the basic magistrates table in

154

the Magistrates Courts Act 1952, schedule 3. The first amendment had come in the Criminal Justice Act of 1967, s. 93, which had set imprisonment for non-payment of fines at 14 days for fines not exceeding £5 and 30 days for fines not exceeding £20. The second amendments came in the Criminal Law Act of 1977, s. 59. Imprisonment for non-payment of fines was set at 7 days for fines not exceeding £25 and 14 days for fines not exceeding £50. In conclusion, then, whereas fines were increased, the length of sentences for non-payment of fines was reduced.

Appendix 2

THE RESEARCH PROGRAMME

Although a research programme to compare and contrast the centres ideally would have collected identical information at each centre, it should be obvious from the profiles of the centres that their clientele, staffing, facilities and methods were so varied, that similar measures could not be reproduced exactly in each center, as they were not always applicable or appropriate.

The research aimed to assess how far each centre achieved or attempted to achieve each of the goals associated with detoxification. Thus the similarities and differences between the functions of each setting were traced by assessing which of these functions were *intended* to be carried out, as ascertained from the operational policy and management studies of the staff, and to what extent they were *actually* carried out, as ascertained by systematic research monitoring.

The Leeds centre received a more extensive investigation than was possible in the other centres. The Leeds study was used, to some extent, as a pilot study for the other centres; it was considered unnecessary to replicate the collection of all of the information gathered in Leeds both because some of the information gathered was found to be of limited or no value for the purposes of this research. An overall package was evolved from the Leeds study, a modified form of which was used in the other centres. Naturally, the forms used to collect this information varied slightly across centres, and use was made of information previously collected and analysed by the staff in the centres, in order to minimise replication. However some of the existing research, although on similar lines, was not of a form suitable for comparison with information collected at the other centres by the research team.

Research package

The package used at each centre consisted of:

Staff functioning

Staff goal exercise The goal and priorities of each detoxification centre as defined by its staff were elicited using a group exercise run by DEP staff and adapted from management training techniques (Otto and Armstrong, 1977). At Portsmouth, where the numerous staff of four different wards were involved, it was only possible to interview individual staff members.

Staff interviews   Samples of staff were interviewed by DEP staff to find their (the staff's) perception of the goals of the detoxification centre and of their role, what they liked and disliked about their work, as well as what improvements or changes would facilitate what they did, and what supervision they received.

Staff questionnaires   In all centres except Manchester, samples of staff completed an amended version of the Alcohol and Alcohol Problems Perception Questionnaire (AAPPQ) developed by Cartwright (1978).

Client interviews
Samples of clients were interviewed using a standardised schedule. Each interview included the following four sections:

Client characteristics – a structured questionnaire asking for basic demographic variables, employment, education, medical, criminal, social and drinking history.

Current functioning – this gave details of client's accommodation, employment, source of income, health and eating habits in the seven days prior to his/her admission.

Client activities – giving details of any tasks within a detoxification centre for which a client was responsible, and details of client's activities during his/her spare time.

Severity of alcohol dependence – a scored questionnaire based on the concept of the 'alcohol dependence syndrome' and developed by Hodgson, R. *et al.* (1978) and Stockwell, T. *et al.* (1979). The questionnaire assessed the severity of a client's physical and psychological 'dependence' on alcohol along five dimensions. This allowed comparison not only across centres but also with previously examined populations of psychiatric patients labelled as alcoholics.

Client interviews could not be undertaken until the staff of the detoxification centre considered the client well enough to undergo the interview which took between three-quarters of an hour to one hour. Usually clients were not sufficiently well before the third day of their stay. Unfortunately, some clients left before this and thus were not interviewed. Some of the clients thus missed were interviewed during a subsequent admission. (Early leaving was a recurrent problem only at Leeds.) Questionnaires in all cases were delivered verbally and completed by research assistants since when piloting these forms it was found that some clients were unable to read and write.

Services provided
The services provided by each centre were monitored intensively over 12 weeks in Manchester, Oxford, Tower Hamlets and Portsmouth and 9 weeks in Leeds. A shorter time period was used in Leeds due to the greater number of clients passing through the centre. The centre staff and/or the research assistants completed the following forms for all the clients in the centre during the monitoring periods.

Apprehension form   The need to gather details of arrests of drunkenness offenders of course only arose at the designated centres, i.e. Leeds and Manchester. At Leeds, an 'apprehension form' was completed by police officers who brought the client to the detoxification centre, to collect details of time and place of apprehension, mode of transport to the detoxification centre and offence for which the client was apprehended. At Manchester similar questions were added to the 'Crim Sec 26' Form which police officers completed for Home Office statistics upon bringing a drunkenness offender to the detoxification centre.

Admission form   Designed to collect data on times of admission and the process of admission, i.e. if the client was detained in the admitting area and for how long, if the client was medically checked, what physical problems there were, and any medication and other responses provided. The form had to be completed by different personnel across the centres according to their various staffing levels and procedures. At Leeds and Portsmouth, responsibility for clients upon admission lay with an admitting nurse who therefore completed all the forms, whilst at the other three centres responsibility was shared between nurses, who therefore completed part of the form, and, at Manchester, a receptionist responsible for taking administrative details from patients upon admission, at Oxford, a doctor, and at Tower Hamlets, a care assistant.

Daily check form   Designed to collect data on a client's state, any medication prescribed, or any medical attention given on a daily basis. Although some of the events listed would only be likely to happen once during a client's stay, e.g. seeing a chiropodist, it was nevertheless found much more reliable during piloting at Leeds to collect all the possible information on a daily basis, since retrospective listings after a client was discharged led to too many omissions. Again different people had to complete this form across centres because of their various working situations. In Manchester and Portsmouth the forms were all completed by nurses, at Tower Hamlets by nurses in conjunction with care assistants, in Oxford by nurses and doctors, and at Leeds where therapeutic responsibility was most spread across staff groups, it proved most practical for the research assistant to complete the form at the daily staff meeting.

Social work monitoring form Designed to collect data on the length and frequency of client/social worker contact and the nature of the contact in terms of the types of problems dealt with. The form was completed directly by social workers at Manchester and Tower Hamlets, and by the research assistant and social workers at Leeds. Social workers were not employed at Oxford, while at Portsmouth not enough responded to allow for a workable sample.

Discharge form Designed to collect information on the nature of discharge, discharge destination and any arrangements made for follow-up. The form was completed by nurses at Portsmouth, nurses and doctors at Oxford, and care assistants at Tower Hamlets. The information was collected at Leeds by interviews with social workers and at Manchester the form was not used because one of the research doctors was covering this topic.

The bulk of monitoring information was derived from the admission and daily check forms which were standard and applied in all five centres. Social work monitoring forms applied in each centre except Oxford, where the staff felt it was inappropriate for their style of work, whilst in Manchester, the staff felt that the form did not allow for their community work, and thus an extra monitoring form, a 'community social work' form, was also applied. The discharge form did not apply in Manchester since this had been studied by a member of the centre's staff.

Admissions
Data relating to lengths of stay and frequencies of admission was collected, and analysed for a three-year period at each of the centres.

Description of the detoxification centre and its content
(1)   A description of the nature, structure and functioning of the centre was compiled by each research assistant.
(2)   A description of related local specialist and non-specialist facilities was compiled by the research assistant from directories and personal contacts.
(3)   Minutes of meetings of local agencies concerned with collaboration and liaison with the detoxification centres were collected and analysed as described earlier in the text.

Patient screening
St James Hospital at Portsmouth was a psychiatric hospital which did *not* have any special setting to carry out detoxification. Obviously, then, it represented a departure from the other four research designs which were all geared to populations all considered to be requiring detoxification. Initial concern at Portsmouth was rather to define a cohort of persons who were being detoxified, and persons who might have been in need of detoxification treatment, i.e. the

initial part of the research was more concerned with problem identification than service provision.

It would have been inaccurate just to study patients with a diagnosis of alcoholism or alcohol dependence, since their reason for admission might have been some other psychiatric problem and they might not have required any form of detoxification treatment. For example, they might have been abstinent from alcohol for some time before admission. On the other hand, it was assumed that there must have been patients admitted with acute and/chronic problems from drink whose primary diagnosis might be some classification other than an alcohol-related one. In some cases, drinking problems might have gone unrecognised while the patient was in hospital. Obviously all admissions to the special alcohol treatment unit were considered as persons who might potentially require detoxification, but in the general admission wards, screening methods had to be adopted to identify patients at risk of requiring detoxification. This sample was selected by two main methods: (1) a blood test to collect evidence of physiological effects of alcohol. Blood samples were collected by venepuncture as soon as possible after admission from consenting patients. From this were derived:

(a)   Blood alcohol level.

(b)   Mean corpuscular volume (MCV). The indicative value of red blood cell mean volume as a guide to alcohol abuse has been reported by Unger, K. W., and Johnson, D. *American Journal of Medical Science* 267, pp. 281–9, 1974.

(c)   Gamma glutomyl transpeptidase (GGTP) – generally regarded as the liver enzyme most sensitive to alcohol metabolism (Rosalki, S. B. and Rau, D. *Clin. Chem. Acta.* 39, pp. 41–47, 1972). This provides evidence of liver damage due to alcohol and is generally thought to be a good indicator of recent heavy consumption, though not sensitive to heavy consumption some time before the test. It required slightly more blood than usual to be taken.

Any patients with an elevated GGTP and any with a positive alcohol score upon admission were included in the at risk population. Although the mere fact of having alcohol in the blood upon admission might seem a wide criterion, in fact it is relatively unusual for persons to enter hospital having recently been drinking. In fact, very few persons within the sample had any positive indication of alcohol in the blood, and these tended to be somewhat high counts. In addition, all but one patient so identified had other indications of having a drink problem from other parts of the overall screen.

(2)   The research assistant applied a screening questionnaire to each patient admitted. Patients were included in the at risk sample if they answered yes to either of the following questions:

'Do you feel that drinking is causing you problems at the present time?'

'Have you had a recent period in which you have been drinking heavily?'

Patients were also included in the at risk sample if they were implicated by the CAGE questionnaire (Mayfield, D. M. and Johnston, R. G. M., 1980).

Each patient was asked four CAGE questions:

'Have you ever felt you should cut down on your drinking?'

'Have people annoyed you by criticising your drinking?'

'Have you ever felt bad or guilty about your drinking?'

'Have you ever had a drink first thing in the morning to steady your nerves or to get rid of a hangover?'

A positive answer to two or more items has been shown to be a strong indicator that the respondent has a serious drinking problem.

Appendix 3

1   The initiative to set up a centre, or to extend existing services, can come from any number of agencies or individuals. In fact it is usually the non-statutory sector that first points out a gap in services and campaigns for the resources to fill it.

2   Wherever the initiatives spring from, it is vitally important that once a possible need is recognised by district or regional health authorities or social services, a joint working party is set up to assess the need in detail and to draw up recommendations as to the nature and structure of the services required and the staffing and resource implications.

The key members of a working party would be representatives from:

(a)   The district or regional health authority, depending on the size and population distribution in the area.

(b)   Social services; particularly from the field-work department and research and development.

(c)   Any specialist treatment units in the area.

(d)   Non-statutory or voluntary agencies working with the homeless and/or problem drinkers. If few such agencies exist, contact could be made with national co-ordinating bodies such as the Federation of Alcoholic Rehabilitation Establishments, the National Association for the Care and Resettlement of Offenders, the National Council on Alcoholism and the National Cyrenians.

(e)   Any agency for the co-ordination of work with problem drinkers and/or the voluntary sector, should there be one.

(f)   The police.

(g)   The probation service.

Given that members of such a working party are usually heavily committed elsewhere, the appointment of a secretary seconded to the working party to organise meetings, send out papers and to collate information when necessary is recommended.

3   The brief of the working party would be to consider the following: what are the immediate and long-term needs of prospective

clients and what types of acute and chronic problems will they present? Factors to be considered in estimating local needs would be:

(a)   the level, type and distribution of drunkenness offending;
(b)   the size and nature of the single homeless population;
(c)   the provision and scope of existing services for problem drinkers and the homeless;
(d)   the inappropriate use of existing facilities and the demand and excessive pressures on existing health and social services by persons arriving intoxicated and/or requiring detoxification;
(e)   the nature of the geographical area, for example, whether it is rural or urban.

4   Visits to existing centres and services would assist working party members in their work and if resources allow, it would be desirable for existing centre staff to attend working party meetings for discussion of specific items. Use, too, might be made of the knowledge of detox research workers, thus ensuring that the implications of the research are fully understood and explored.

5   Once a statement of need, resources and a strategy for development is drawn up, it is then up to the health authority and social services department to decide on the appropriateness of allocation of finance, given their priorities. If the provision of a centre is regarded as a priority and is likely to be funded, the proposals should be sent to the Home Office and DHSS for their comments.

Should a centre be regarded as a priority but sufficient funds are not available, a number of alternative strategies might be considered. An approach might be made to the DHSS for part or all of the funding on a pump-priming basis or for at least the capital costs; revenue costs might be reduced by nursing and social work staff being seconded as opposed to being paid for from a separate budget. It also might be possible to keep capital costs low by leasing the building from local health or housing authorities. It is not unusual for authorities in inner city areas to have properties available; the rent and conversion required would not be excessive as nothing special or elaborate is required.

However, whatever means are negotiated to get resources, care should be taken to ensure that the type of centre required is viable because of them, not despite them.

6   When funding has been obtained, detailed consideration should be given to the goals and operational policies of the centre. The centre should establish what it is trying to achieve as precisely as possible.

7   Once having clarified the goals of the centre and their relationship to the resources available, the operational policies should be

reviewed so as to ensure that the roles of staff are realistic, the target population is clearly defined and that co-operation and liaison can be fully developed and maintained. It is also recommended that meetings are held with staff of associated agencies to clarify their expectations of the centre and to work out specific procedures for assessment and referral on, etc.

8   A statement of goals must incorporate:
(a)   the target population;
(b)   the referral procedures into the centre;
(c)   selection criteria;
(d)   the provision and type of immediate help for clients on arrival;
(e)   the overall orientation of the medical and social services provided;
(f)   prescribing policy;
(g)   the number of staff members required, their roles and level of participation in decision making;
(h)   the structures for support, supervision and training of staff
(i)   referral out;
(j)   the provision of follow-up
(k)   re-admission policy;
(l)   co-operation and liaison with other relevant agencies and parts of the detox service;
(m)   monitoring and record-keeping procedures.
     Furthermore, any centre, however it is defined, must be able to manage persons in the state of intoxication and withdrawal and attend to the associated immediate physical and psychological problems of persons in that state.

9   Throughout the life of a centre it is important to integrate and evaluate. What a centre tries to achieve must be determined by existing provision and scale of other local services relevant to the target population. Both these services and the type of scale of need in an area may change over time. The centre should, therefore, continually monitor the needs of clientele, its responses and its relationships to other services, and be prepared to redefine its goals and methods.

Appendix 4

WEILER REPORT (1971): RECOMMENDATIONS FOR
DETOXIFICATION SERVICES

'Detoxification, diagnosis and assessment

90. Special arrangements for detoxification will be indispensable to any future system which attempts to deal comprehensively with public drunkenness, though we would not wish to see the further consideration that may be necessary before they can be provided delay the implementation of our other recommendations (paragraphs 15.1 and 15.53).

91. Persons who under present arrangements would be arrested for being drunk in public should be taken by the police to special detoxification centres and there detained while they are dried out and any necessary medical and social investigation is carried out (paragraph 15.14).

92. The police should retain their discretion whether or not to take criminal proceedings subsequently in these cases. It would seldom be appropriate, however, to prosecute in circumstances calling only for a charge of drunk and incapable. We would also expect that in cases calling for some other drunkenness charge or a minor non-drunkenness charge, the police, as experience of the system developed, would increasingly exercise their discretion by not proceeding with the charge (paragraphs 15.20 to 15.22).

93. The proposed detoxification centres, and the procedures involved in the process of detoxification, diagnosis and assessment, should have statutory authority (paragraph 15.25).

94. The initial period of detention should not exceed 72 hours but there should be provision for a further period of detention not exceeding seven days for persons diagnosed as having a serious drinking problem requiring further investigation (paragraphs 15.26 to 15.30).

95. Detoxification centres should be demonstrably medical and social work facilities with a clearly therapeutic purpose. They should be under medical direction with 24 hour medical cover.

Nursing and social work staff will also have a key part to play. Staff training at all levels will require careful planning (paragraphs 15.32 to 15.40).

96. The establishment of fully operational detoxification centres will be possible only in a few cities where the extent and pattern of drunkenness offences warrant it. Elsewhere the service will have to be provided in other less specialised ways (paragraph 15.43).

97. We estimate that in the inner London area the number of detoxification centre places needed on any one night might vary between a minimum of 125 and a maximum of about 450. In Birmingham the need is likely to vary between a minimum of 20 places and a maximum of 80 places (paragraphs 15.44 to 15.47).

98. There would be considerable advantages if a pilot scheme could be mounted as a basis for experiment and research in advance of the legislation required for the establishment of statutory detoxification arrangements. There are, however, practical and legal difficulties about this. If these could be overcome we would suggest that one experimental centre be situated in inner London and another in a city outside London with a significant number of habitual drunken offenders (paragraphs 15.48 to 15.51).'

Habitual Drunken Offenders: Report of the Working Party, HMSO

Select Bibliography

ADVISORY COMMITTEE ON ALCOHOLISM. *The Pattern and Range of Services for Problem Drinkers*, Report to DHSS and Welsh Office, HMSO, 1978.

ANNIS, H. M. 'The detoxification alternative to the handling of public inebriates: the Ontario experience', *Journal of Studies on Alcohol*, 40, pp. 196–210.

ANNIS, H. M. *et al. Task Force II. Report on the Operation and Effectiveness of the Ontario Detoxification System*, Addiction Research Foundation, Ontario, 1976.

CARTWRIGHT, A. K. J. 'The Effect of Role Insecurity on Therapeutic Commitment of Alcoholism Counsellors', unpublished PhD thesis, Institute of Psychiatry, University of London, 1978.

CARTWRIGHT, A. K. J. 'The attitudes of helping agents towards the alcoholic client: the influence of experience, support, training and self-esteem', *British Journal of Addiction*, 75, pp. 413–431, 1980.

CARTWRIGHT, A. K. J., SHAW, S. J., and SPRATLEY, T. A. *Designing a Comprehensive Community Response to Problems of Alcohol Abuse*, Maudsley Alcohol Pilot Project, DHSS, 1975.

DEPARTMENT OF HEALTH AND SOCIAL SECURITY. *Community Services for Alcoholics*, Circular 21/73, HMSO, 1973.

GROSS, M. M. 'The Psycho-biological Contributions to the Alcohol Dependence Syndrome' in Edwards, G. *et al.*, *Alcohol Related Problems*, WHO Offset Publications No. 32, Geneva, 1979.

HAMILTON, J. R. 'Detoxification of Habitual Drunken Offenders', University of Edinburgh, unpublished MD thesis, 1976.

HAMILTON, J. R. 'Detoxification: The First Step' in Madden, J. S., Walker, R. and Kenyon, W. H. (eds), *Alcoholism and Drug Dependence: A Multi-disciplinary Approach*, Plenum, New York, 1979.

HAMILTON, J. R. 'Evaluation of a detoxification service for habitual drunken offenders', *British Journal of Psychiatry*, 135, pp. 28–34, 1979.

HODGSON, R. *et al.* 'Alcohol dependence: the concept, its utility and measurement', *British Journal of Addiction*, 73, pp. 339–342, 1978.

167

JELLINEK, E. M. 'Phases of alcohol addiction', *Quarterly Journal of Studies on Alcohol*, 13, pp. 673–684, 1952.

JELLINEK, E. M. *The Disease Concept of Alcoholism*, Hillhouse Press, Highland Park, New Jersey, 1960.

MAKANJUOLA, J. 'A Follow-up Study of Police Referrals to the Manchester Detox Centre', PhD thesis, University of Manchester, 1981.

MAYFIELD, D. M. and JOHNSTON, R. G. M. 'Screening Techniques and Prevalence Estimation in Alcoholism in *Phenomenology and Treatment of Alcoholism*, Spectrum Books, 1980.

ORFORD, J. *Evaluation of Detoxification Centres: A Review of the Literature*, prepared for the Department of Health and Social Security Homelessness and Addictions Research Liaison Group, unpublished, 1982.

OTTO, S. J. and ARMSTRONG, F. *The Action Research Experiment*, South East London Consortium, 1978.

OTTO, S. J. and ORFORD, J. *Not Quite Like Home: Small Hostels for Alcoholics and Others*, Wiley and Sons Ltd, 1976.

ROSALKI, S. B. and RAU, D. 'Serum gamma-glutamyl transpeptidase activity in alcoholism', *Clinica Chimica Acta*, 39: 41–47, 1972.

ROYAL COLLEGE OF PSYCHIATRISTS. *Alcohol and Alcoholism: The Report of a Special Committee of the Royal College of Psychiatrists*, Tavistock Publications Ltd, 1979.

SHAW, S. J. 'The Rising Prevalence of Alcohol Problems Amongst Women' in Camberwell Council on Alcoholism, *Women and Alcohol*, Tavistock, 1980.

SHAW, S. J. 'What is Problem Drinking?' in Plant, M., *Drinking and Problem Drinking*, Junction Books, 1982.

STOCKWELL, T. *et al.* 'The development of a questionnaire to measure severity of alcohol dependence', *British Journal of Addiction*, 74, pp. 79–87, 1979.

UNGER, K. W. and JOHNSON, D. 'Red blood cell mean corpuscular volume: a potential indicator of alcohol usage in a working population, *American Journal of Medical Science*, 267: 281–289, 1974.

WEILER, T. G. *Habitual Drunken Offenders: Report of the Working Party*, HMSO, 1971.

Index